Commercial Printing Guide

ALDUS ®

ALDUS. PAGEMAKER.
Version 5.0 / Apple. Macintosh. / Microsoft. Windows™

ALDUS PAGEMAKER® COMMERCIAL PRINTING GUIDE

Version 5.0 for use with Microsoft® Windows™ and Apple® Macintosh® computers

FIRST EDITION
February 1993

COPYRIGHT

©1993 Aldus Corporation. All rights reserved. No part of this publication may be reproduced, transmitted, transcribed, stored in a retrieval system, or translated into any language in any form by any means without the written permission of Aldus Corporation.

SOFTWARE LICENSE NOTICE

Your license agreement with Aldus Corporation, which is included with the product, specifies the permitted and prohibited uses of the product. Any unauthorized duplication or use of Aldus PageMaker 5.0, in whole or in part, in print, or in any other storage and retrieval system is prohibited.

GOVERNMENT RESTRICTED RIGHTS LEGEND

Use, duplication, or disclosure by the Government is subject to restrictions as set forth in subparagraph (c)(1)(ii) of the Rights in Technical Data and Computer Software clause at DFARS 252.227-7013 and paragraph (d) of the Commercial Computer Software - Restricted Rights at FAR 52.227 - 19. Subcontractor/Manufacturer is Aldus Corporation, 411 First Avenue South, Seattle, Washington 98104-2871.

LICENSES AND TRADEMARKS

Aldus, the Aldus logo, PageMaker, and PrePrint are registered trademarks, and OPI, PressWise, TIFF, and TrapWise are trademarks of Aldus Corporation, and PhotoStyler is a registered trademark of U-Lead Systems licensed to Aldus Corporation. Adobe Photoshop, Adobe Type Manager, SuperATM, and PostScript are trademarks of Adobe Systems, Inc, which may be registered in certain jurisdictions. All references to PostScript on the screen or in this guide are references either to the PostScript interpreter or to PostScript language. Apple and Macintosh are registered trademarks and TrueType is a trademark of Apple Computer, Inc. Color Art is a trademark of Fuji Corp. Cromacheck and Cromalin are registered trademarks of DuPont. Crosfield is a registered trademark of Crosfield Design Systems. DCS is a trademark of Quark, Inc. Linotype-Hell is a trademark of Linotype-Hell AG. Microsoft and MS-DOS are registered trademarks and Windows is a trademark of Microsoft Corp. PANOSE is a trademark of the typeface matching system from ElseWare Corporation. ElseWare Corporation takes no responsibility for the mapping results of fonts that do not also bear the PANOSE trademark.

PANTONE® is a registered trademark of Pantone, Inc. PANTONE®* Computer Video simulations used in this product may not match PANTONE-identified solid color standards. Use current PANTONE Color Reference Manuals for accurate color.

*Pantone, Inc.'s check-standard trademark for color. ©Pantone, Inc., 1986, 1988. Pantone, Inc. is the copyright owner of PANTONE Color Computer Graphics and Software, which are licensed to Aldus Corporation to distribute for use only in combination with Aldus Corporation software. PANTONE Color Computer Graphics and Software shall not be copied onto another diskette or into memory unless as part of the execution of Aldus PageMaker.

PC is a trademark of International Business Machines Corp. PKZip is a registered trademark of PKWare, Inc. Scitex is a registered trademark of Scitex Corporation, Ltd. Stuffit is a trademark of Aladdin Systems, Inc. Suitcase is a trademark of Fifth Generation Systems, Inc. TOYO is a trademark of TOYO Ink Mfg. Co., Ltd. Trumatch is a trademark of Trumatch, Inc. Other product and corporate names may be trademarks or registered trademarks of other companies, and are used only for explanation and to the owners' benefit, without intent to infringe.

Portions of graphics filters © Access Softek 1990-1993. Color Database © Dainippon Ink and Chemicals, Inc. licensed to Aldus. Portions of MGX filter © Micrografx, Inc. 1985-1992. All rights reserved. TRUMATCH 4 Color Selector © 1992 Trumatch, Inc. XyWrite filters © 1985-1992 Aldus Corporation. All rights reserved. Portions ©1988-1991 XYQUEST Corporation. All rights reserved. Portions of the WordPerfect Macintosh Filter 1988 WordPerfect Corporation. All rights reserved. The WordPerfect Macintosh filters are licensed by WordPerfect to Aldus Corporation.

ALDUS PAGEMAKER AND MICROSOFT WINDOWS

Aldus PageMaker operates in a graphics environment called Microsoft Windows, created by Microsoft Corporation. An extension of the MS-DOS operating system, Microsoft Windows gives a standard look and feel to Aldus PageMaker and all other Windows applications.

To run Aldus PageMaker under Microsoft Windows, you need to license and install Microsoft Windows.

ALDUS PAGEMAKER AND THE APPLE MACINTOSH

SYSTEM UTILITIES AND TOOLS ARE COPYRIGHTED PROGRAMS OF APPLE COMPUTER, INC., LICENSED TO ALDUS CORPORATION TO DISTRIBUTE FOR USE ONLY IN COMBINATION WITH ALDUS PAGEMAKER. APPLE SOFTWARE SHALL NOT BE COPIED ONTO ANOTHER DISK (EXCEPT FOR ARCHIVAL PURPOSES) OR INTO MEMORY UNLESS AS PART OF THE EXECUTION OF ALDUS PAGEMAKER. WHEN ALDUS PAGEMAKER HAS COMPLETED EXECUTION, APPLE SOFTWARE SHALL NOT BE USED BY ANY OTHER PROGRAM.

APPLE COMPUTER, INC., MAKES NO WARRANTIES, EITHER EXPRESS OR IMPLIED, REGARDING THE ENCLOSED COMPUTER SOFTWARE PACKAGE, ITS MERCHANTABILITY, OR ITS FITNESS FOR ANY PARTICULAR PURPOSE. THE EXCLUSION OF IMPLIED WARRANTIES IS NOT PERMITTED BY SOME STATES. THE ABOVE EXCLUSION MAY NOT APPLY TO YOU. THIS WARRANTY PROVIDES YOU WITH SPECIFIC LEGAL RIGHTS. THERE MAY BE OTHER RIGHTS THAT YOU HAVE WHICH VARY FROM STATE TO STATE.

Aldus Corporation	Aldus Europe Limited	Aldus Pacific Rim
411 First Avenue South	Aldus House	411 First Avenue South
Seattle, Washington 98104-2871	West One Business Park	Seattle, Washington 98104-2871
U.S.A.	5 Mid New Cultins	U.S.A.
Tel. 1 206 622 5500	Edinburgh, Scotland	Tel. 1 206 622 5500
	United Kingdom, EH11 4DU	
	Tel. 44 31 453 2211	

For service and support in the United States, please contact Aldus Corporation. For service and support in Africa and Europe, please contact Aldus Europe Limited. For service and support in Canada, South America, and East Asia, please contact Aldus Pacific Rim. Outside these areas, please contact your local distributor or dealer. If you purchased your Aldus software through a hardware manufacturer, technical support for your software may instead be provided as part of the system support from the hardware manufacturer.

ISBN 1-56026-172-2 (Macintosh)
ISBN 1-56026-161-7 (Windows)
Printed in USA
989-177

PageMaker and the Prepress Process

This book explores the processes and issues involved in preparing color PageMaker publications for reproduction on a commercial printing press—a set of tasks known as the prepress process.

Until recently, most prepress tasks—such as scanning color photographs, trapping, and generating process-color separations—were performed exclusively by highly skilled specialists working on expensive proprietary systems. The introduction of Aldus PageMaker in 1984, and the desktop publishing revolution that followed, changed that.

Aldus and PageMaker have continued to respond to the needs of the publishing industry so that today it's possible to complete many prepress tasks, such as printing color separations, from the desktop.

The flexibility and direct control offered by this new technology present challenges as well. Deciding whether to handle prepress tasks yourself using PageMaker or to leave them to prepress professionals (who may use a combination of desktop and traditional tools) involves weighing a complex set of variables. This book will help you understand the variables, make sound decisions about your working processes, and meet these new challenges. We want you to make the most of the freedom and flexibility of Aldus PageMaker while anticipating and avoiding problems as you produce your publications.

Contents

Color and commercial printing: an overview

Basic color theory, key color printing terms, and an overview of reproducing a color publication on a commercial printing press.

Planning for commercial printing

How to work with printing and prepress service providers—service bureaus, separation facilities, and commercial printers—to print a PageMaker publication successfully.

Creating a publication

What to consider as you make key decisions about setting up a publication, specifying colors, importing graphics, working with scanned images, managing fonts, and trapping objects.

Printing separations

Key options for printing separations from PageMaker, including information about screen rulings and angles and tips for handing off files; plus overviews of printing separations from post-processors and the proofing process.

Special topics

Adding custom page sizes and font names to custom PostScript printer description (PPD) files and creating custom color libraries.

PageMaker is a powerful tool that makes it easy to design and produce your publications. Preparing publications for commercial printing takes careful thought. Both imagesetters and commercial printing presses have inherent limitations, and it's all too easy to create publications that are difficult to print on either an imagesetter or a printing press. By thinking of your design and production cycles as steps in a larger process, you can make choices that will let you work more efficiently and help you achieve the best printed results.

We created a poster for a fictitious furniture company named VIA 1.618 to use as an example throughout this book.

Sketch your design ideas

Gather all of the requirements for the publication, including budget, audience, and schedule, before you start to work. Then, working with pencil and paper or directly on your computer, rough out your initial design ideas.

Talk to your printer and prepress service provider

Select a commercial printer and prepress service provider (commercial printer, service bureau, or separation facility) early in the design process, so that they can help you plan a successful color printing job. Share your design ideas and ask questions before you create your publication.

Lay out your publication

Create your publication in PageMaker, including setting up the publication pages, specifying and applying colors, importing images, and preparing to print the separations. If your design includes photographs, consult with your prepress service provider to determine how to scan them.

Review and proof your publication

Print composite or preproof copies of your PageMaker publication on any black-and-white or color desktop printer. Once you print film separations, use industry-standard proofs, such as 3M MatchPrint or DuPont Cromalin, to check color quality and safeguard against production problems.

Print color separations

Decide whether to print separations from PageMaker or using a post-processor. Then, provide your prepress service provider with your PageMaker publication in its native file format or as PostScript files to print the separations on an imagesetter or to manipulate them in a post-processing application.

Color and commercial printing: an overview

When you create a color publication in PageMaker, you want the colors in the final printed piece to match your expectations as closely as possible. Yet matching colors closely is one of the most difficult tasks in commercial printing. To accomplish your goal, you need three things—a fundamental understanding of color and how it's displayed and printed on different devices, clear knowledge of the commercial printing process, and close communication with your commercial printer.

This chapter presents basic color and commercial printing concepts. Chapter 2, "Planning for Commercial Printing," discusses how to work with a commercial printer. We also recommend browsing in your local library, bookstore, or art supply store for books on graphic arts and commercial printing. The more you know about printing color, the better you can prepare your publications for printing.

The properties of color

How we perceive color, the models we use to describe color, and the ranges of color different devices can display or print.

Printing terminology

Definitions of basic commercial printing terms.

Commercial printing

How a publication is reproduced on an offset printing press.

Common printing problems

Common problems that occur in commercial offset printing.

Objects appear to be certain colors because of their ability to reflect, absorb, or transmit light, which we perceive as color. Our eyes are sensitive enough to perceive thousands of different colors in the spectrum of visible light—including many colors that cannot be displayed on a color monitor or printed on a commercial printing press.

We describe color in terms of three characteristics—hue, value, and saturation. Hue is the name of the color, such as orange, pink, or green. Value (also called lightness) indicates the darkness or lightness of a hue—in other words, how close it is to black or white. Saturation (also called chroma) refers to the vividness or dullness of the hue.

Many environmental factors, such as changes in lighting or the proximity of colors to each other, influence our individual perception of these color characteristics. In general, differences in how we perceive colors don't seriously affect our lives. In the realm of commercial printing, however, differences in how we perceive colors often affect the success of the print job. Understanding how different factors influence your color perception and what factors determine printed colors will help you manage printing results.

Every device used to create a color publication—be it a scanner, color monitor, color desktop printer, or commercial printing press—reproduces a different range of color in the visible spectrum. You can view many more colors on your monitor than you can print on a desktop printer or a commercial printing press. In addition, scanners and color monitors use a different color model to describe color than that used by desktop printers and commercial presses. As colors move from the screen to the printing press, they're converted from one color model to the other—so you don't get in print exactly the same colors you see on the screen.

When designing publications to be printed on a commercial printing press, think in terms of what can be reproduced with ink on paper and not what you see on your monitor. In addition, you'll need to specify and proof colors carefully. By working closely with your commercial printer and mastering some basic color concepts, you'll be able to print color publications that meet your expectations.

Color Perception

Many factors subtly influence your color perception. In the underlying art, we used only one background color—blue—yet the blue appears to change because the different colored lines overlapping it affect your perception of the color.

Color Models

Additive color model

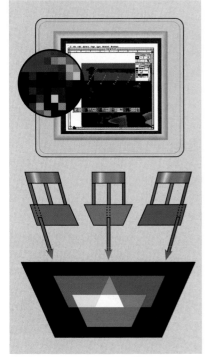

You can combine varying intensities of three wavelengths of light—red, green, and blue (RGB)—to simulate the range of colors found in nature. Red, green, and blue are called the **additive primaries**. If you combine 100% of red, green, and blue, you perceive the color as white. If none of the additive primaries are present, you perceive black.

Subtractive color model

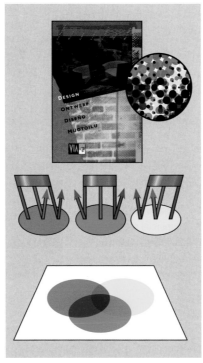

If you subtract red, green, or blue from white light (a 100% intensity of red, green, and blue), you create cyan, magenta, or yellow (CMY). For example, you perceive an object as cyan if it absorbs (subtracts) 100% red light and reflects green and blue. These colors are called the **subtractive primaries**, and form the basis for printed process colors.

Why are two models used to describe color? Because different media manipulate light in different ways. Video technology (for example, computer monitors, scanners and television screens) uses the additive RGB model: it transmits light which we perceive as different colors. In commercial printing, however, translucent cyan, magenta, and yellow inks are printed on a page. (Printers use a fourth ink, black, to deepen shadows and to print true black type and lines.) These inks absorb and reflect light—we perceive the reflected light as different colors.

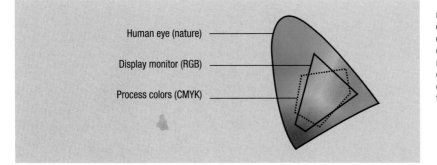

Human eye (nature)

Display monitor (RGB)

Process colors (CMYK)

The visible spectrum contains millions of colors. While the color gamuts (the range of colors a device can reproduce) for different devices used in commercial printing overlap, they don't match exactly. Therefore, one cannot completely re-create the other.

Continuous-tone art

If you look closely at an original black-and-white or color photograph, you'll see that the image consists of solid shades of gray or color that blend smoothly. An original photograph is called continuous-tone art.

Halftone screens

To reproduce continuous-tone art on a commercial printing press, the image must be broken into a series of dots of various sizes and colors, called a halftone screen. In electronic publishing, scanning is the first step in converting continuous-tone art to halftone screens. A commercial printer uses black dots to re-create black-and-white images and cyan, magenta, yellow, and black dots to re-create color images on the press. Small dots create light areas and large dots create darker areas.

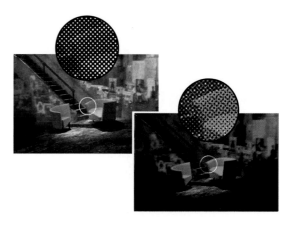

Spot colors and tints

Spot colors are printed on a printing press with premixed, semi- or fully-opaque inks. (You can choose from among hundreds of different spot-color inks.) You use spot colors to achieve an exact color match—in a corporate logo, for example—or to add visual impact to a one-, two-, or three-color publication for a nominal cost.

A tint is a lightened color. You create a tint by controlling the number and size of the dots used to print the color; this is called screening the color.

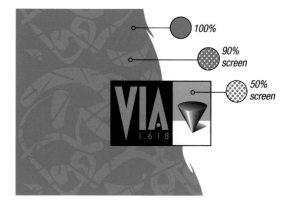

100%

90% screen

50% screen

Process colors

Process colors are created by printing overlapping dots (halftone screens) of cyan, magenta, and yellow (CMY) inks to simulate a large number of different colors. Since CMY inks are translucent, they absorb some colors and reflect others. To create blue, for example, you combine cyan dots (which absorb red and reflect blue and green) and magenta dots (which absorb green and reflect blue and red). Your eyes merge the cyan and magenta dots to perceive the color blue. You can use process colors to simulate spot colors and to reproduce color images.

You could, in theory, mix 100% of cyan, magenta, and yellow to create black. However, you never print 100% of these inks for two reasons: (1) Inks are imperfect and printing this combination of cyan, magenta, and yellow creates a muddy brown color instead of a sharp black. (2) Printing too much ink on a particular area of a page oversaturates that area, causing the quality of the printing to deteriorate. To achieve fine detail and strong shadows in print, printers use black ink (K) along with cyan, magenta, and yellow inks (CMYK).

Undercolor removal and gray-component replacement (UCR and GCR)

Using black ink in process-color production solves a particular printing problem—that 100% of the three CMY inks does not produce a true black. However, adding black ink causes other printing problems, such as excessive ink on the page. To correct this problem, printers use undercolor removal (UCR) and gray-component replacement (GCR) to reduce the amount of cyan, magenta, and yellow ink and to compensate for the additional black ink.

If you are scanning images yourself, you can use a product such as Aldus PrePrint or Aldus PhotoStyler to adjust the UCR and GCR settings for an image. If a prepress service provider scans the images for you, work with that vendor and your commercial printer to determine the amount of UCR and GCR to specify for the particular printing conditions.

Separations

To print continuous-tone color art on a commercial printing press, you first separate the page containing the composite art into its component colors by printing a film separation for each ink—cyan, magenta, yellow, black, and any spot colors—needed to print the colors in your publication. (Spot-color separations are also called spot-color overlays.) Your printer uses these film separations to create the printing plates used on the press.

Knocking out and overprinting

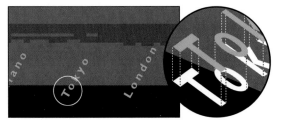

Light type is knocked out of a dark background...

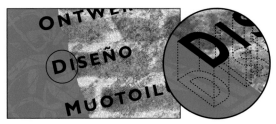

...whereas black type is overprinted.

When you print overlapping colors in PageMaker, the top color knocks out the color beneath it by default. In other words, the top color prints and any colors positioned behind it do not print where the top color overlaps them. Imported graphics, such as TIFF or EPS files, also knock out colors or objects that are positioned behind them, unless object-level overprinting was specified in the illustration program. Typically, you want colors and objects to knock out so that the overlapping colors don't blend to create undesired colors.

You can specify colors and certain PageMaker-drawn elements (lines, rectangles, and ellipses) to print on top of (overprint) elements behind them; as a rule, you should always overprint black text. Commercial printing is an imperfect process, so you sometimes use techniques such as overprinting to prevent small gaps from appearing between colors or objects as a result of misregistration on the printing press.

Open Prepress Interface (OPI)

OPI is a standard extension of the PostScript page-description language that provides a way for page-layout programs to describe the way scanned images are used. The large file sizes of scanned image files present challenges to desktop publishers: transporting these files is difficult, and manipulating them can be inordinately slow. When you work with an application that supports OPI, such as PageMaker, you design your pages with a placeholder image. When you print the publication as a PostScript file to give to a prepress service provider, OPI comments are included to specify the placement, sizing, and cropping of any TIFF images in the file. The prepress service provider then automatically links to the high-resolution version of the image before printing your separations, saving time and minimizing stripping and rework costs.

Trapping

Art that hasn't been trapped can easily misregister on the press, causing gaps, or light leaks, to appear between adjacent elements.

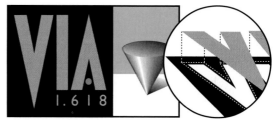

Trapping compensates for misregistration by slightly overlapping adjacent elements.

To create the results you want, a commercial printer must print inks in succession in register—exactly aligned with each other. If one or more inks print out of register, you may see gaps between color objects or places where a process ink stands out rather than appearing to blend with the other inks to simulate a color. To minimize the effects of misregis-tration, commercial printers developed trapping, a technique in which adjacent colors slightly overprint. You can create traps in PageMaker, in an illustration program (such as Aldus FreeHand), or your prepress service provider can use Aldus TrapWise to trap your PageMaker pages and any art they contain.

You can choose any of four different processes to print a publication: gravure, silkscreen, flexography, or offset lithography. The method you choose depends on your budget, your choice of commercial printers, and the printed results you want. Because offset lithography is the most popular printing process, we use it here to explain the basics of commercial printing. For more information on other types of printing, consult a commercial printer.

Offset lithography involves printing from a flat surface and works on the principle that oil and water do not mix. The printing plate holds ink because the image area is treated to be receptive to the oil-based ink but not to water—not because the image area is raised (as in letterpress) or etched (as in gravure).

A multicolor offset press has a separate printing unit for each ink being printed. If, for example, you're using process colors and one spot color in a print job and your commercial printer's press can handle five colors, a printing unit will be set up for each ink—cyan, magenta, yellow, black, and the spot color. The paper will then pass through each unit in succession. If the press handles fewer colors, your printer will print two or three inks first, stop the press and reset the inks, and then run the paper through again to print the other inks.

Step 1: Platemaking

Using a photographic process, a printer exposes the reversed image from the film separation (a negative) onto a flat metal or paper plate, and then develops the plate. The image area of the plate, now a positive so you can read it, has a chemical coating that attracts ink but repels water. The non-image area has a coating that attracts water and repels ink.

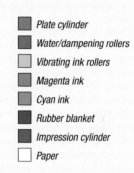

A printing press repeats the wetting, inking, offsetting, and printing steps over and over throughout the print run.

■ Plate cylinder
■ Water/dampening rollers
□ Vibrating ink rollers
■ Magenta ink
■ Cyan ink
■ Rubber blanket
■ Impression cylinder
□ Paper

Step 2: Wetting

The plate is mounted on a rotating cylinder. When the press starts, the plate comes into contact with water rollers first. Dampening solution (water plus additives) flows constantly from a traylike fountain through a series of rollers to the plate cylinder. The last water roller wets the entire printing plate, except where the plate has been treated to resist water.

Step 3: Inking

Next, the ink roller applies oil-based ink to the plate. Thick, greasy ink flows from another fountain through a series of vibrating rollers, which distribute the ink evenly and thinly. When the last ink roller contacts the wet printing plate, it smoothly distributes ink across the water-resistant image area.

Step 4: Offsetting

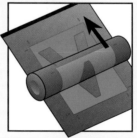

The final roller is a rubber blanket, which is pressed against the printing plate and carries away a reversed inked image (the offsetting step). The rubber blanket has some flexibility and gives slightly when pressed against paper, so the image can transfer evenly to both smooth and textured paper.

Step 5: Printing

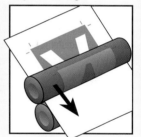

In the last step, the paper—in individual sheets (sheet-fed) or on a continuous roll (web-fed)—passes between the rubber blanket and an impression cylinder. The inked blanket cylinder with its reversed image presses against the paper, thus printing the positive image.

Rosette patterns and moirés

When you print process-color separations, the rows of dots (halftone screens) for each process-color ink are printed at a specific angle so that the ink dots don't print on top of each other. Instead, they form a symmetrical pattern, called a rosette pattern, which your eye easily merges into smooth color gradations.

If a process-color ink prints at an incorrect angle or if the paper shifts as it passes through the printing press, the rosette pattern does not print correctly. Instead, an unsightly moiré pattern appears, which disrupts your perception of smooth color gradations.

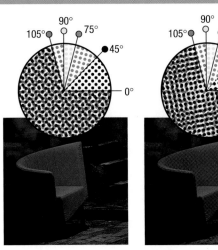

Rosette pattern   Moiré

Misregistration

Paper sometimes stretches and shifts as it absorbs moisture and is pulled through a press. This causes multicolor jobs to print out of register (colors misalign) and results in two problems in your final printed work: slight gaps between overlapping colors and moiré patterns in process colors. Trapping can help you compensate for misregistration.

Registered   Misregistered

Halftone dot gain

Many variables, from the photomechanical processes used to produce separations to the paper type and press used, affect the size of printed halftone dots. Typically, dots increase in size (dot gain) as wet ink spreads under pressure from the rubber blanket. (Dots may also increase in size as negatives from different sources are reprinted to produce the final film.) If too much dot gain occurs, images plug up and colors (such as spot-color tints) print darker than specified. Your printer can help you compensate for dot gain.

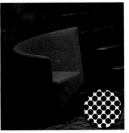

Halftone dots in a color proof…   …the same image after printing.

"What leaves us at the end of the day is a disk..." says Nick Bellenberg, Editorial Systems Project Manager at IPC Magazines, Ltd., in London.

IPC publishes 57 magazine titles, the largest of which circulates 1.5 million copies weekly, and has 45% of the market in the United Kingdom. Nevertheless, the publication process at IPC is similar to that at much smaller operations. Unlike many large publishers, IPC does not own production facilities. Film imaging, traditional prepress work, and printing are all contracted out.

This dependence on outside service providers makes communication critically important to meeting deadlines. Bellenberg and Neil Bailey, Editorial Systems Manager, specialize in maintaining the link between the company and its service providers, and they work to bring their knowledge of the external service environment into the company. They also look for ways to streamline the publishing process, which often means doing more of their own color work. "The line in the sand has shifted toward in-house production," says Bailey.

Here are their tips for working with a service provider:

- Avoid converting spot colors, especially those defined in the color libraries included with PageMaker, to process colors.

- Ask the provider how best to set up a publication, especially if you use nonstandard page sizes. Depending on the provider's hardware configuration, you may be able to make special considerations to save film costs.

- Tell your commercial printer what types of images you're using and decide up-front if you will incorporate them electronically or have them stripped in manually. PageMaker provides OPI links to high-end systems, so you can use a low-resolution image in PageMaker and then have your service bureau link to the high-resolution version. Sometimes, however, it makes more sense to strip in images manually (as when you use black-and-white photos, which are relatively inexpensive to strip in, or when your printing schedule is tight, as it is in magazine production).

- Take advantage of the service provider's system capabilities. For example, IPC uses tint blocks that are percentages of cyan ending in 9 (19%, for example) as picture placeholders. The Scitex system can then search for cyan tints of that percentage and automatically knock them out.

- On some systems, printing black text on top of a process-color background can produce a halo if misregistration occurs. IPC avoids this problem by defining the text color as 100% black plus the CMY percentages of the background color, in effect forcing the black to overprint the background color. Ask your service provider if this is necessary with their equipment.

- Discuss any bleeds with your service provider, and ask what size bleed is appropriate for their equipment.

- In general, think in terms of layers, just as you would using traditional pasteup: Everything except the images is on the foreground layer. You see the images through windows that you create on this foreground layer.

Every commercial printing job requires you to consider a complex set of variables ranging from what your budget and schedule allow to how the paper stock and printing press affect your printing job. The earlier you think about these variables, the more control you'll have over the quality, price, and schedule of your project.

In addition to choosing a commercial printer, you may need to select prepress service providers to print color separations and to handle trapping and stripping. Several types of vendors can provide prepress services: prepress houses and color trade shops; color-capable imagesetting service bureaus; and commercial printers. Shop for vendors who are willing to answer your printing questions, and ask to see samples of their work. The quality of your separations is critical, so select a separation facility carefully.

Choose your vendors early, and make them a central part of your design team. Review your rough design ideas with them, discuss any potential printing problems, and identify prepress tasks and who's responsible for them.

Talk to your commercial printer

Questions you should be ready to ask or answer when you work
with a commercial printer.

Talk to your separation facility

Questions to ask the vendor printing your color separations.

Talk to your commercial printer

Be ready to answer questions about:

- your budget and schedule

- the number of copies you plan to print

- the dimensions of your publication

- the colors you specified—spot, process, or both

- your choice of paper (weight, texture, and color)

- your choice of finishing (if any)

- your use of bleeds (art that goes beyond the edge of the page)

- the graphics in your publication (whether you imported them or want them manually stripped in)

Ask your own questions. For example:

✔ **What experience does the commercial printer have working with electronic publishing jobs?**

✔ **What color-matching systems does the commercial printer support?** PageMaker 5.0 includes five color-matching libraries: Dainippon, Focoltone, PANTONE MATCHING SYSTEM, TOYO, and Trumatch.

✔ **Is your choice of paper readily available or does it need to be ordered?** What is the minimum quantity? How expensive is it?

✔ **How will your paper choice (its finish and so on) affect your design?**

✔ **Which prepress tasks will the commercial printer do?** Decide who is responsible for tasks such as stripping photos, adding screens, and camera work.

✔ **What prepress tasks, such as creating spot-color overlays, might be more cost-efficient if done traditionally?**

✔ **What parts of the design might require trapping?** Who's responsible for it?

✔ **Who checks the quality of the film separations and troubleshoots film or press problems?** How will dot gain, UCR, and GCR be handled?

✔ **What color-proofing systems are available to use?**

✔ **How much will the job cost?** How long will it take once the commercial printer has the final separations?

Also, always ask about the printing press:

✔ **Is it a sheet-fed or web-fed (continuous roll) press?** Web presses tend to show more dot gain, so you may want the commercial printer to work with the separation facility to compensate for dot gain in the separations.

✔ **How many colors can be printed in one press run?** On a two-color press, your four-color job will require two press runs. You may be able to cut costs by shopping for a commercial printer with a four-color press.

✔ **In what order will the spot and process inks be printed?** If you want a spot-color ink to overprint another ink, you may need to specify the sequence in which the inks are printed.

✔ **Can you save money by making a minor design change?** For example, would slightly changing the dimensions of the publication in order to print three-up (three pages per press sheet) instead of two-up yield significant savings?

Finally, ask how to print the separations:

✔ **How should the separations be printed: on paper or film?** For some designs, it's more cost-effective to perform certain prepress tasks and shoot the final film separations from paper separations. When your file contains halftone screens, always print to film.

✔ **If you're providing film separations, should they be positive or negative, and with the film emulsion up or down? What screen ruling should be used?** The answers to these questions depend entirely on the type of press your commercial printer will use, so don't make any assumptions. Always ask.

✔ **Is a final composite print of the publication required for reference? What type?** Some commercial printers can use a black-and-white composite print marked with color information, while others may require a color composite. Separations printed to a desktop printer may provide additional information for the commercial printer.

Ask how to set up your files to print on an imagesetter:

✔ **What kind of imagesetter does the separation facility use?** In Windows, you must select the correct printer type and resolution when you set up the PageMaker publication. If you don't have a PPD file for a particular imagesetter installed on your hard drive, the separation facility should provide it for you.

✔ **Who sets which printing settings?** Be very specific when you talk about these settings; many separations must be reprinted because of lack of communication about printing settings.

✔ **How should you deliver your PageMaker file: as PostScript files, as a regular PageMaker publication, or both? How will linked files be managed?** Some vendors prefer PostScript files that include linked graphics so they can print files quickly. Many others prefer to have the publication and any linked files so they can double-check your print settings and troubleshoot problems directly.

✔ **At what resolutions can the separations be printed?** Color separations need to be printed at a high enough resolution to get the quality you want; printing less complex pages at an intermediate resolution may save you money.

✔ **What fonts are available to print your publication?** To avoid font substitution, you must either use the same fonts (from the same font vendor) as the separation facility or include font information when you print the publication as a PostScript file to disk.

Check quality control:

✔ **How often are the imagesetters calibrated? What steps are taken to ensure their precision?** A knowledgeable separation facility will calibrate its imagesetters often—typically both daily and every time the film is changed. The imagesetter should be calibrated for the density of the emulsion on the film and for the halftone dot value, and operators should verify that film processing chemicals are not depleted. Less experienced separation facilities may only calibrate for the halftone dot value.

✔ **Who is responsible for checking the film?** Someone must verify that the film is clean and in good condition, that it is not scratched, that all separations printed for each page, and that the film registers. See "Checking your film separations" on page 64 for more information.

Rules of thumb

- Choose a reputable service bureau, color separation facility, and commercial printer.
- Be organized and communicate with your vendors often.
- Expect the unexpected and print tests to a desktop printer along the way.
- Note your decisions on a checksheet or in a read-me file to hand off to the commercial printer with your final files.

Why assume the responsibility of doing electronic prepress on the desktop when there are professionals who do this work full-time? Johnny Sutton, customer liaison at R.R. Donnelly's Greensboro (North Carolina) Graphics Service Center, cites two reasons: to meet tight turnaround schedules and to reduce costs.

Doing desktop layout, including color work, does save both time and money—if it's done right. A prepress service provider can help. "For us it's a training issue," Sutton says. "Most of our customers want to do it. We show them how to make the tools do what they want to do.

"With every new customer, we look at sample pages, then give them back, along with some constructive criticism. We show the customer how they built the pages, and how the pages should be built. Sometimes, we even build parallel electronic and mechanical pages and compare the results. It can take awhile to get a customer to the proper comfort zone," says Sutton.

This educational service is not unique to Donnelly. Many printers provide such training, even if customers then use what they learn to take more of the prepress work back to the desktop. Sharing knowledge is the answer, says Sutton: "If customers don't build their pages properly, we both suffer."

Much of what Sutton tells customers derives from his own work habits in high-end prepress work. In particular, working with layers and laying out pages more precisely than is necessary with traditional mechanicals are two practices that carry over to the Macintosh, he says.

Here are Sutton's most popular tips:

- Use the best graphic format for the job. Logos, for example, should be EPS line art, which is resolution-independent; scanned bitmaps can look jagged when printed, especially if resized.

- Use TIFFs as FPO (for position only) art, so you can suppress printing the placeholders automatically, either to link to high-resolution versions of the art in a separation program such as Aldus PrePrint, or to strip the art in traditionally. (To suppress printing TIFFs, use the "Omit TIFF files" option in the "Options" printing dialog box.)

- Apply color to an imported graphic only if it is line art, a monochrome, or grayscale TIFF. Although you can apply color to EPS graphics and other types of imported line art, you may not get the results you want. (See "Applying color to imported graphics" on page 33.)

- Make sure the service provider has the fonts from the same foundry (vendor) you are using.

- Always supply your commercial printer with proofs of your work, including proofs from a 300-dpi PostScript printer. Mark any special use of color or other features on your paper proofs and call them to the printer's attention.

Creating a publication

The decisions you make as you create your publication are critical to your success in creating separations and printing your publication on a press. This chapter describes the tools PageMaker gives you to work on color publications and explains general principles to keep in mind as you work.

Setting up a publication

Key options when setting up a publication for commercial printing.

Specifying colors

Specifying custom colors, selecting colors from color libraries, and applying colors to imported graphics.

Imported graphics

Scanning and applying halftone screens to images and managing links to external graphics.

Managing fonts

Managing fonts for your publication.

Trapping

Ensuring that colored objects align on the press, including techniques for trapping and overprinting colors in PageMaker.

Specifying bleeds

Printing colors to the edge of your page.

Setting up a publication for commercial printing

A Page and Page dimensions Select a preset page size for your publication or specify a custom page size up to 42 inches by 42 inches (1066.8mm by 1066.8mm).

Before specifying large custom page sizes, ask your prepress service provider about the maximum page size that you can print on their imagesetters. If, for example, you're printing at 1200 dots per inch on an Agfa SelectSet 5000, the maximum dimensions you can print are 15.7 inches (399mm) by 22 inches (559mm).

B Orientation Specify whether your publication's pages will be taller than they are wide, or vice versa. This setting determines the default for the orientation setting in the "Print document" dialog box. If you make your publication pages wide but select tall when you print, part of each page will not print. For more information, see "Choosing the right paper size" on page 56.

C Compose to printer (Windows only) Before you start to work, select the type of printer on which you will print the final copy of your publication so that PageMaker will compose your publication to the capabilities of that printer. Fonts, resolutions, and predefined paper sizes are printer-specific, and composing to the wrong printer type may cause problems at print time. (This setting replaces the "Target printer..." command in PageMaker 4.0 for Windows.)

Note: You do not have to have the final printer physically connected to your computer to select it, but you do need to have the correct printer driver installed under Windows. For more information on installing printer drivers, refer to the *Microsoft Windows User's Guide*.

D Target printer resolution Select the resolution at which you'll print the final version of your publication. Ask your prepress service provider to recommend a resolution.

The printer resolution affects how PageMaker resizes monochrome bitmap images. If you change the resolution after resizing bitmap images using the Printer-resolution-scaling option on the Control palette or magic-stretch, be sure to resize them again once you specify the final printer resolution and before you print separations.

For more information...

Windows

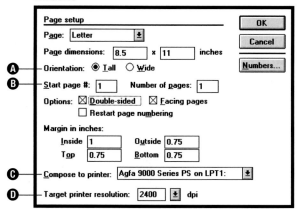

A — Orientation: ◉ Tall ○ Wide
B — Start page #: 1 ...

Key "Page setup" options

The "Page setup" dialog box opens when you start a new publication, so you can specify the page dimensions and target printer resolution before you begin working. For Windows, the "Compose to printer" option is critical, as it defines what fonts will be available.

Macintosh

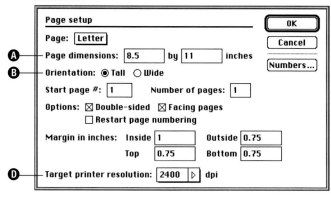

Tip

PageMaker for the Macintosh relies on the Apple LaserWriter 8.0 printer driver (or the Adobe PSWriter driver) to print on PostScript printers. This printer driver is installed when you install PageMaker; be sure to use it to set up a PostScript printer before you print. Refer to the "Print…" command description in the *PageMaker 5.0 User Manual* for more information.

Choosing spot or process colors

Whether you use spot colors, process colors, or both in
your design depends on your budget, the purpose of the
publication, and the types of objects in the design. Some
general guidelines:

- Determine how many colors you need to use. Using
  spot colors is more cost-effective if you're printing three
  or fewer colors, while using process colors is more cost-
  effective when printing four or more colors.

- Choose colors that reinforce your goals. Are you trying to
  reflect a certain mood or elicit a particular response?

**Ask yourself these questions when deciding what type
of colors to specify:**

A   Are you planning to import color images? You'll need to
use process colors to reproduce these images.

B   Do you need to match other colors, such as a particular
red that appears in a photo in your publication or a color
in an illustration? Matching spot colors to existing work
is difficult and usually increases the cost of a job.

C   Do you need to meet precise color standards, such as
including a corporate logo that uses a particular spot
color as part of its identity? If so, you'll need to use spot
colors or some combination of spot and process colors.

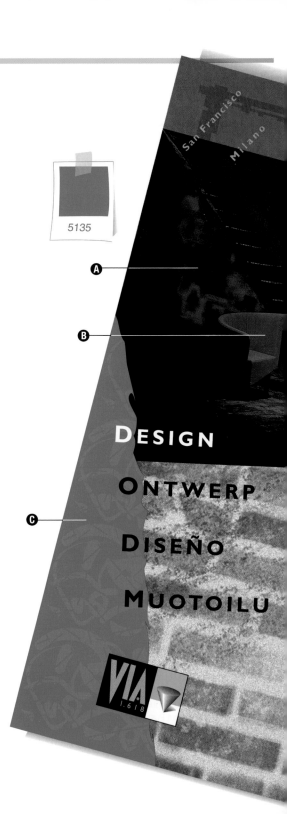

For more information...

Tips for working with process colors

C 0-100 + M 0-100 + Y30

- To achieve predictable printed results, always use the CMYK (cyan, magenta, yellow, and black) values provided on printed color charts to specify process colors, or select colors from one of the process-color libraries included with PageMaker. (You can get printed custom color charts from most commercial printers.) Do not specify colors based on their appearance on your computer screen. Printing presses can reliably reproduce only a fraction of the colors visible on a 24-bit color monitor.

- Most printers recommend a maximum ink coverage of 250%-320%, so that the paper doesn't become oversaturated and stretch or tear. Oversaturation increases the likelihood of misregistration.

- Use a single, solid ink (such as 100% black or a dark spot color) to print hairline rules and small text. Fine elements printed with two or more colors are difficult to print in register.

- Do not override the screen rulings and angles specified in the PPD files and displayed in the "Color" printing dialog box. These settings are designed to minimize moiré patterns when printing process colors.

- If you plan to convert spot colors to process colors, use the "Edit color" dialog box to convert each color individually rather than using the "All to process" option in the "Color" printing dialog box. Selecting "All to process" converts all spot colors (even those in EPS files) to process, making it impossible to print a combination of spot- and process-color separations.

- PageMaker can edit the spot colors in imported EPS files, giving you more control over the number of separations required to print your publication. In addition to editing the colors and converting spot colors to process, you can turn spot colors into tints of PageMaker colors (to force them to print on the same separation).

Tip

PageMaker's process black overprints text by default, but knocks out all other objects. Tints and other colors defined in PageMaker knock out by default.

Matching colors precisely is difficult. From the lighting in which you view the colors to the quality of the printing plates and the craftsmanship of the printer, there are too many variables for total control.

Balancing two approaches to color printing may help you get acceptable results. First, learn to accept compromises with your commercial printer and to focus on managing the variables, rather than agonizing over the elusive exact color match. Second, take advantage of color-matching systems that let you achieve more predictable results.

Pantone, Inc. released the first color-matching system more than 30 years ago and dramatically improved designers' ability to get the spot color results they wanted. Now, as the demand for color printing grows, more vendors are marketing reliable systems that let you specify colors more precisely than before. PageMaker includes five color-matching libraries from which to choose colors. For information about creating a custom color library, see page 72.

Note: Consult with your commercial printer about which color libraries they support and recommend.

Color-matching libraries included with PageMaker

Library name	Type	Number of colors	Description
Dainippon	Spot	1280	Colors organized into three categories—gay and brilliant; quiet and dark; grays, metallics, and basics.
Focoltone	Process	763	Colors organized by whether they share a common percentage of either cyan, magenta, yellow, or black and will, therefore, minimize trapping requirements.
PANTONE	Spot	736	The industry standard for specifying spot-color inks.
PANTONE	Process	3006	Colors organized in chromatic order. Includes process-color simulations of the spot-color library.
TOYO	Spot	1050	Colors organized first by hue and then by saturation.
Trumatch	Process	2093	Process colors specified in small CMYK increments to avoid color gaps.

For more information...

▶ To apply color to an imported graphic

PageMaker lets you override the colors in certain types of imported graphics with colors defined in PageMaker. The graphics will print with the applied color either as composites or on separations. RGB TIFF, CMYK TIFF, and DCS files always print with their original colors, so applying color to these images has no effect.

Original file

EPS graphic

Grayscale TIFF image

Select the graphic and click on a color on the "Colors" palette. You can apply colors to EPS graphics, monochrome and grayscale bitmap graphics, PICT and PICT2 files (Macintosh), and Windows Metafiles.

On-screen color

EPS graphic with color applied in PageMaker

Grayscale TIFF image with color applied in PageMaker

The color selected on the "Colors" palette is the applied color. Colors applied to monochrome and grayscale TIFF images, PICT graphics, and Windows metafiles display on-screen. Colors applied to EPS and PICT2 graphics do not display on-screen.

Printed color

Printed EPS graphic after applying a color in PageMaker

Printed grayscale TIFF image after applying a color in PageMaker

The graphic prints with the applied color. When you apply a process color and then print separations, the graphic prints on the separations required to produce the process color. For spot colors, the graphic prints on the spot-color separation for the applied color.

▶ To remove an applied color

Select the graphic and choose "Restore original color" from the Element menu. The graphic prints and appears on-screen with the colors it had when you first placed it in PageMaker.

```
Element
  Line                        ▶
                              ▶

  Define colors...
  Restore original color

  Link info...
  Link options...
```

In traditional publishing, a printer prepares photographs for printing by creating halftones that are manually stripped into place in the separations. To incorporate a photograph or slide into a PageMaker publication electronically, you first convert it to a monochrome, grayscale, or color TIFF file by:

• scanning the photo or slide on a desktop scanner.

• having a prepress service provider scan the photo or slide on a high-end drum scanner.

When you work with a prepress service provider to scan continuous-tone art, the prepress technician will determine the best scan resolution to use given the paper stock and screen ruling you'll use to print your final publication (when scanning line art, always scan at the highest possible resolution). When you do the scanning yourself, you can apply one of two simple formulas to determine the best scan resolution. To use the formulas, you need to know:

• the original height and width of the image.

• the final uncropped height and width of the image (if you plan to resize the image in PageMaker).

• the screen ruling you'll use to print the image.

Note: A higher scan resolution (measured in pixels per inch, or ppi) does not always give superior printed results. In fact, unnecessarily high scan resolutions increase the size of the files and cause longer print times without improving the printed results.

Determining grayscale and color scan resolutions

$$\text{screen ruling} \times 2 = \text{scanning resolution}$$

Use this formula if you are not resizing the imported image in PageMaker.

$$(\text{final image height} \div \text{original image height}) \times \text{screen ruling} \times 2 = \text{scanning resolution}$$

Use this formula if you are resizing the imported image in PageMaker.

Note: Multiplying the screen ruling by 2 is a conservative approach, and may result in scanning at too high a resolution. It's possible to multiply the halftone screen ruling by as little as 1.5 and still get good results.

Sample scanned images

Scan resolution: 200 ppi
File size: 80k
Screen ruling: 150 lpi

Scan resolution: 350 ppi
File size: 230k
Screen ruling: 150 lpi

Although the file sizes of the two images above differ, the printed image quality is consistent.

Scanning tips

75 ppi | 100 ppi | 150 ppi | 200 ppi | 350 ppi

Slices of this image were scanned at different resolutions and printed with a screen ruling of 150 lpi. Pixelation is more visible at lower scan resolutions.

- Use the highest possible scan resolution when you scan line art on a desktop scanner.

- Save scanned images as TIFF files for the best printed results.

- Speed up printing of images scanned at too high a resolution on low-resolution desktop printers by eliminating unnecessary image data. Select "Optimized" in the "Options" printing dialog box before you print. Always select "Normal" when printing at high resolutions.

- Determine what your quality requirements are in the beginning. Desktop scanners provide a quick, inexpensive means of creating color TIFF images, but they may not provide the quality you need. Discuss other scanning options with your prepress service provider.

- To print separations of RGB TIFF images from PageMaker, you must either: (1) Open the RGB TIFFs in an image-manipulation program, such as Aldus PrePrint or Adobe PhotoShop, and convert them to CMYK TIFF or DCS files, which PageMaker can place and separate, or (2) use a post-processor, such as Aldus PrePrint, to print the separations of your PageMaker PostScript files.

Scan resolution: 300 ppi
File size: 360k
Screen ruling: 75 lpi

Scan resolution: 300 ppi
File size: 360k
Screen ruling: 150 lpi

When there's sufficient scan image data, the screen ruling determines how fine or coarse the printed image appears.

The final printed quality of a grayscale TIFF image is not determined by scanning resolution alone. Also important are:

- the screen ruling at which the halftone image is printed. (Screen ruling is measured in lines per inch—lpi—or the number of halftone dots in a row one inch long.)

- the resolution of the imagesetter or desktop printer (dpi) used to print the halftone image.

The screen ruling determines the size of the halftone cells that make up the image; the printer resolution determines the number of printer dots that print in each cell, and therefore the number of grays used to reproduce your image. To print a visually convincing halftone image, you need to print about 150 shades of gray.

For more information about optimized screens and screen rulings, see "Choosing screen rulings and screen angles" on page 54.

The optimized screen selected in the "Color" printing dialog box determines the default screen ruling used to print scanned images. To override this value for a specific image, use the "Image control..." command on the Element menu.

Halftone dots

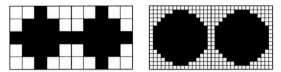

These halftone cells are printed with the same screen ruling but different printer resolutions. The left cell contains 25 printer dots and can reproduce 26 shades of gray. The right cell contains 256 printer dots and can reproduce 256 shades of gray.

Screen rulings for grayscale images

$$(\text{printer resolution} \div \text{screen ruling})^2 + 1 = \text{printed shades of gray}$$

To calculate a screen ruling that will produce the results you want at a given printer resolution, use this simple formula.

Recommended screen rulings

At this printer resolution (dpi)	Use this screen ruling (lpi)	To print this many grays
300	53-60	26-33
600	71-85	51-72
1200/1270	65-128	89-256
2400/2540	90-150	256
3386/3600	150-300	128-256

Note: 256 is the maximum number of grays you can produce in PostScript.

Tips for managing links

- Don't delete externally linked graphics or you will be unable to print a high-resolution version of the image. If you move an externally linked graphic to another volume, reestablish the link in the "Links" dialog box.

- Remember to hand off externally linked files to your prepress service provider. See "Handing off your publications" on page 57 for more information.

- Before printing your publication, use the "Links…" command to verify that you are using the most up-to-date version of all imported files.

- Decide at the outset of your project whether you'll store graphics internally or externally, and set your "Link options" defaults accordingly. If you're working with small graphics, store them internally. Large graphic files are best stored externally.

Links		OK
Document	**Kind**	**Page**
Brick wall.tif	TIFF	1
Texture.tif	TIFF	1
Torn page.eps	Encapsulated PostScript	1
? VIA chairs.tif	TIFF	1
VIA logo.eps	Encapsulated PostScript	1

Status : PageMaker cannot locate the linked document. Use the 'Info…' dialog to find the document.

[Info…] [Options…] [Unlink] [Update] [Update all]

This externally linked file can't be located. Until the link is re-established, PageMaker will print the low-resolution placeholder you see on-screen.

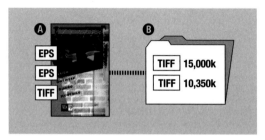

In our sample poster, smaller bitmaps and EPS files (A) are stored internally, while color TIFF images (B) are externally linked.

PageMaker automatically stores some placed elements, including text, within a publication. You can choose to store imported graphics either internally or externally by setting link defaults in the "Link options" dialog box. Whether an imported object is stored internally or externally, you can use the "Links…" command to determine whether the original file has been modified and to update it if it has, so the correct version of the imported object always prints. Managing your links is a key part of successfully printing your publications.

When you store a graphic internally, PageMaker includes a complete copy of the graphic file in your publication. Storing graphics internally increases your publication files size by the amount of each internally stored graphic, but a high-resolution version of the file is always available when you print.

When you link externally to a graphic, PageMaker places a low-resolution screen version of the graphic in your publication file as a placeholder. When you print the publication, PageMaker locates the original graphic file on disk and uses it to print the graphic. Linking externally minimizes your publication file size, but if the original file cannot be located, the low-resolution placeholder prints, probably yielding disappointing results.

Knowing how fonts are made available and printed from PageMaker can help you avoid problems when printing your publication. This section outlines the variables that control fonts on your computer.

Choosing the type of font to work with is the first step in making sure the type on your pages displays and prints correctly. Competing font standards make this an important decision: the same typeface design may be available as a PostScript font and as a TrueType font. Because their visual characteristics are subtly different, using one type of font for displaying and proofing your work and then using a different type for printing can cause unpleasant surprises. If you're working with a service bureau, ask for a recommendation.

PostScript fonts are the industry standard for quality. Although most PostScript fonts exist for both the Macintosh and Windows, fonts are handled quite differently in each environment. When you work with the same publication on both platforms, the PANOSE Typeface Matching System (included with PageMaker) or SuperATM can automatically respecify fonts.

Anatomy of a PostScript font

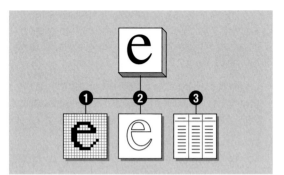

PostScript fonts consist of three parts: (1) the screen font, (2) the printer (or outline) font, and (3) the information used to compose the font (or the font metrics).

Macintosh

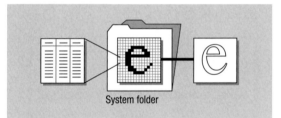

System folder

On the Macintosh, a font is available in PageMaker when the screen font is properly installed. Font metric information is stored in the screen font, so a separate font metrics file isn't used.

Windows

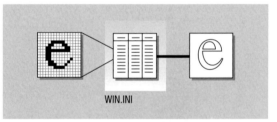

WIN.INI

In Windows, a font is available in PageMaker if the font is listed in the printer driver for the selected target printer or if the font metrics file-name is listed in the target printer's section in the WIN.INI file. Screen fonts in Windows are optional, and aren't necessary if you use a type manager, such as Adobe Type Manager (ATM).

Printing downloadable PostScript fonts

Some printer fonts are built into, or resident on, your printer and therefore print automatically. When you purchase additional typeface designs, the associated printer fonts must be downloaded, or sent, to the printer. PageMaker uses the information in the PPD file for the printer type selected in the "Print document" dialog box to determine whether to download PostScript fonts.

PageMaker reads the PPD file that you select at print time:

- **If the font is listed in selected PPD,** PageMaker assumes the font is available on the printer and doesn't download it.

- **If the font is not listed in PPD but the printer font is available to be downloaded,** PageMaker downloads it.

- **If the font is not listed in PPD and is not available to be downloaded**, PageMaker substitutes the printer's default font (usually Courier) at print time.

Troubleshooting common font problems

Macintosh problems

- **Type appears on screen and prints with spacing that is obviously much too loose or much too tight. When another font is applied, the problem is corrected.** The screen font, which contains font spacing information, is damaged. Remove, and then reinstall the font.

- **Text incorrectly prints as Courier on an imagesetter.** The font you specified was not listed in the PPD file for the selected printer type and was not available in the proper place to be downloaded. If the font is resident on the printer, see "Creating a custom printer file" on page 71. Otherwise, move the printer font file to a location where it can be found and downloaded.

Windows problems

- **Certain fonts aren't available on PageMaker's Type menu.** The wrong target printer is selected. The printer you select in "Compose to printer" in the "Page setup" dialog box determines which fonts will be available for use in your publication. In Windows, most types of fonts are installed for a specific printer and port combination.

- **Downloadable fonts used in your publication don't print properly.** If only the PFM file is listed in the WIN.INI file for a downloadable font, PageMaker assumes the font is available at the printer and doesn't download it. To correct this problem, either reinstall the font or manually update the WIN.INI file to include a reference to both the PFM file and the printer font file. Refer to your *Microsoft Windows User's Guide* for more information.

When the inks used for adjacent objects print out of register, unsightly gaps or color shifts appear between the objects. Trapping compensates for misregistration by slightly overlapping adjacent objects.

Traditionally, trapping is a prepress task handled by a commercial printer. Although it's possible for designers to specify traps in PageMaker ("Creating traps in PageMaker" on pages 44-45 provides instructions), leaving this task to prepress professionals is easier and often more cost-effective in the long run, especially when desktop-based prepress tools like Aldus TrapWise are used. TrapWise automates the trapping process, providing improved quality and a cost-effective alternative to manually trapping your PageMaker publications. Discuss using TrapWise with your prepress service provider; for more information about preparing publications for TrapWise, see "Using a post-processor for trapping and imposition" on page 60.

When considering how to trap your publications, begin by talking to your commercial printer about who's responsible for trapping, what needs to be trapped, and, if you assume the responsibility, what size traps to specify.

Registration and trapping

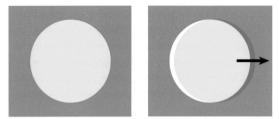

When spot colors print out of register, visible gaps appear between adjacent objects.

Knockouts and overprinting

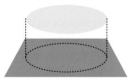

Knockouts preserve the integrity of the colors you specify.

Overprinting two colored objects results in a third, unwanted color.

When you print separations, PageMaker automatically knocks out overlapping objects. In some cases, you may want to overprint two objects, either to create a special effect or to avoid the need to trap overlapping objects. You can specify overprinting for individual fills and lines or for all objects of a specific color.

When process colors print out of register, color shifts may occur.

Spreads and chokes

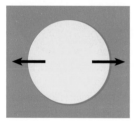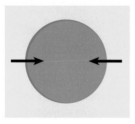

A spread is typically used to trap a light object to a dark background.

A choke is typically used to trap a dark object to a light background.

Spreads and chokes are two types of traps. When two colors meet on the page, the darker color defines the edge of the lighter object. Spreading a light foreground object into a dark background and choking a light background into a dark object minimizes the visual effect of traps.

Your printer should determine the trap sizes (the amount of overlap for each trap) to use for your job. Differences in paper characteristics, screen rulings, and press conditions require different amounts of trap. The guidelines below provide a starting point for printing at these screen rulings on an offset sheet-fed or web press.

Trap size guidelines

Screen ruling (lines per inch)	Trapping values* (inches)	(points)
65	.0077 to .0308	.55 to 2.20
100	.0050 to .0200	.36 to 1.44
133	.0038 to .0152	.27 to 1.08
150	.0033 to .0132	.24 to .96
200	.0025 to .0100	.18 to .72

*The lower value assumes excellent press registration (the press is off by no more than half the distance between a row of halftone dots). The higher value assumes less exact press registration (the press is off by a full row of halftone dots).

You can specify whether individual colors print over as opposed to knocking out underlying colors. Overprinting creates special effects with overlapping colors and can be used to avoid trapping. Object-level overprinting is specified in the "Fill and line" dialog box. You specify color-level overprinting in the "Edit color" dialog box by selecting the name of the color and checking "Overprint."

When you choose to overprint objects or colors, keep these points in mind:

• Overprinting an ink increases the amount of ink coverage on the page, and may cause problems on the press. Before setting inks to overprint, talk to your commercial printer.

• Object-level overprinting overrides color-level defaults. If you set a rectangle to overprint, it will overprint even if the color is set to knock out.

• The default process black ink causes all black graphics—including imported monochrome and grayscale TIFF images, which are black by default—to knock out. Black text, however, overprints by default. Use the "Fill and line…" command to specify whether PageMaker-drawn objects overprint or knock out. To overprint imported images, create a 100% tint based on the color, set the tint to overprint, and apply the tint to the images.

When to overprint colors

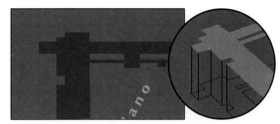

Overprint colored objects to achieve special effects…

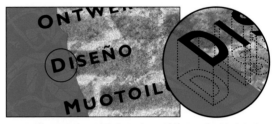

…or use overprinting to eliminate the need for trapping black text.

Overprinting an entire ink color can create interesting design effects while eliminating the need to create traps. Overprinting is especially useful when working with small black text.

To overprint some objects assigned a given color while knocking out others, create a 100% tint based on the color, and set the tint to overprint. Apply the tint to the objects you want to overprint, and apply the color to objects you wish to knock out.

For more information…

PageMaker 5.0 User Manual

Which color is darker?

When trapping colored objects that are similar in hue, it may not be obvious which color is darker and which is lighter (and therefore, which object you should trap). From left, the color swatches on the facing page rank colors from light to dark.

Trapping with a third color

	C	M	Y	K
☐ Foreground object	0	30	100	0
◼ Background object	65	0	23	34
◼ Trap color	65	30	100	34

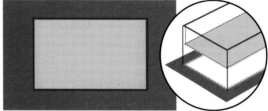

When you create a trap for two process colors, create a third color that you can overprint. Specify the third color by comparing the CMYK values in the two colors and taking the highest percentages of the shared process inks.

Trapping with shared colors

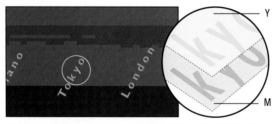

When two adjoining process colors both include some percentage of magenta, any gaps between the objects will be magenta rather than white and will therefore blend more easily.

When working with process colors, you usually create traps for objects that share some common colors by defining a third color based on the shared components; this third color creates a common color bridge between the objects. To avoid trapping problems with process colors:

- Specify and use process colors that share a significant percentage of at least one process ink. If misregistration occurs on the printing press, the gap that appears between the objects will be colored rather than white, so it will be much less noticeable and trapping may not be necessary.

- Consider selecting colors from a process-color library, which can help you handle trapping. When colors in a library are organized by shared tints of a common process-color ink, it's easy to select colors and know they will trap correctly.

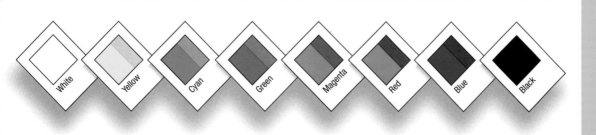

▶ **To create a choke**

1. **Select the dark foreground object.**

2. **Choose "Fill and line…" from the Element menu.**

   In the "Line:" list, select a line weight that is twice the size of the desired trap and then click to select "Overprint" for the line. Click "OK" to close the dialog box. For example, use a .5-point line to create a .25-point trap. When you print the separations, the background object will be choked under the foreground object, creating a trap.

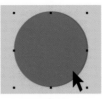

Fill and line		OK
		Cancel
Fill: Solid	Line: .5 pt	
Color: Blue	Color: Blue	
☐ Overprint	☒ Overprint	
	☐ Transparent background	
	☐ Reverse line	

▶ **To create a spread**

1. **Select the light foreground object.**

2. **Display the Control palette.**

   On the Control palette, select the center reference point on the Proxy. Then, increase the "H" and "W" values by twice the amount of the trap size. For example, to create a .5-point trap add 1 point to each dimension. Click the Apply button.

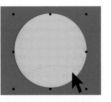

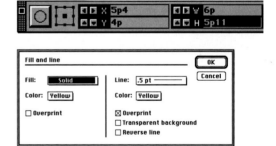

3. **Choose "Fill and line…" from the Element menu.**

   In the "Line:" list, select a line weight that is twice the size of the desired trap and then click to select "Overprint" for the line. Click "OK" to close the dialog box. When you print the separations, the foreground object will be spread over the background, creating a trap.

Fill and line		OK
		Cancel
Fill: Solid	Line: .5 pt	
Color: Yellow	Color: Yellow	
☐ Overprint	☒ Overprint	
	☐ Transparent background	
	☐ Reverse line	

Tip

When you assign a line weight to a PageMaker-drawn box or oval, the thickness of the line is measured in from the perimeter of the object. When you set the line to overprint, PageMaker calculates the stroke from the center of the line, rather than the perimeter of the object. This is important to remember when you're specifying traps in PageMaker, as other drawing programs measure the thickness of the line so that it extends half in and half outside the object.

▶ To trap a grayscale TIFF image to a colored background

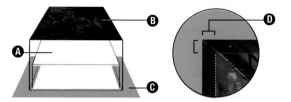

To trap an image to a colored background, place a slightly smaller "[Paper]"-colored rectangle (A) behind an imported monochrome or grayscale TIFF image (B) to create a knockout (C), and then set the color assigned to the image to overprint the background (D).

```
┌─────────────────────────────────────────────┐
│  Create keyline              ┌──────────┐     │
│                              │   OK     │     │
│  Extend │ -.3 │ points outward └──────────┘     │
│                              ┌──────────┐     │
│  ◉ Bring keyline to front of object│ Cancel   │     │
│  ○ Send keyline behind object └──────────┘     │
│                              ┌────────────┐   │
│  ☐ Knock out under keyline   │ Attributes…│   │
│     Overlap interior by │ 0 │ points └────────────┘   │
└─────────────────────────────────────────────┘
```

Use the "Create keyline…" Addition to create a rectangle that is smaller than the selected image by the specified amount and to apply the attributes needed to create a trap. For more information about trapping using the "Create keyline…" Addition, refer to *Aldus PageMaker 5.0 Online Help.*

1. **Select the TIFF and choose "Create keyline…" from the Aldus Additions submenu on the Utilities menu.**

   To create a rectangle slightly smaller than the selected graphic, enter a negative value equal to the trap size for the "Extend" option in the "Create keyline" dialog box. For example, type -.3 to create a .3-point trap. Talk to your commercial printer to determine the ideal trap size for your project.

2. **Click to select "Send keyline behind object."**

3. **Click "Attributes…" to open the "Fill and line" dialog box.**

   Select "Solid" from the "Fill" list, select "Paper" from the "Color" list, and select "None" from the "Line" list. Click "OK" to close the dialog box. Positioning a "Paper"-colored rectangle behind the TIFF image knocks out the colored background behind it; because the rectangle is slightly smaller than the image, the edges of the TIFF overprint the background.

4. **Choose "Define colors…" from the Element menu.**

   Click "Edit…," and set the color assigned to the image to overprint. If you want other like-colored objects to knock out, select "New…" instead of "Edit…" in the "Define colors" dialog box, create a 100% tint of the color assigned to the image, and set the tint to overprint. Then apply the 100% tint to the TIFF image and any other objects you want to overprint rather than knock out. Click "OK" to close the dialog box.

Printing an object to the edge of the final printed piece requires creating a bleed. Bleeds ensure that when the printed paper is trimmed during the finishing process, the ink coverage extends to the very edge of the paper; for example, the colored bars on the side of each page in this book required bleeds.

Although PageMaker places no limits on the size of a bleed you can create, it's a good idea to consult with your printer to determine the minimum bleed size for your job. Common bleed sizes range from $\frac{1}{16}$ inch to $\frac{1}{4}$ inch (3-6mm); in PageMaker, bleeds larger than $\frac{1}{4}$ inch (6mm) may interfere with crop marks and other printer's marks.

When you specify bleeds or printer's marks, remember to specify a paper size at least .875 inch (23mm) larger than the publication's page size.

Note: By default, PageMaker limits bleeds for TIFF images to $\frac{1}{8}$ inch (3mm). Select "Extra image bleed" in the "Options" printing dialog box to print a full image bleed when creating an EPS or a SEP file.

▶ To create a bleed

1. **Extend the object you wish to create a bleed for off the page by the amount of the bleed.**

   The distance an object extends off the page is the size of the bleed.

2. **In the "Paper" printing dialog box, select a paper size that is at least .875 inch (23mm) larger in both dimensions than your publication page.**

   For any page size, select or create a paper size large enough to accommodate printer's marks. For more information, see "Choosing the right paper size" on page 56. To print crop marks and other printer's marks, select "Printer's marks" in the "Options" printing dialog box.

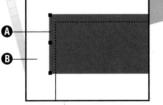

To create a bleed, extend the bleed object (A) onto the pasteboard (B) by up to $\frac{1}{4}$ inch (6mm).

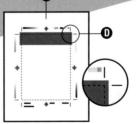

When printed on a paper size (C) large enough to accommodate printer's marks, the bleed object extends beyond the crop marks (D).

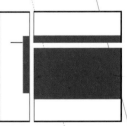

The crop marks indicate where the printed page will be trimmed.

Trapping properly is one of the more demanding tasks of the printing process. Do you do it on the desktop, or let your printer handle it for you? If you trap your work yourself rather than having a prepress house do it, you are responsible for the results, says David Zwang, Principal of the Zwang Consulting Group in Danbury, Connecticut.

A consultant with 25 years of experience in traditional and electronic prepress, Zwang provides advice and training for clients that include design and advertising agencies. "People almost feel that they have to do trapping because they can. But it's not just a matter of having the tools," says Zwang. Doing trapping on the desktop transfers a critical and exacting task from a trained printing professional to the graphic designer or production artist who may have little or no training.

Unlike most work in PageMaker, you can't judge the successfulness of trapping on-screen. The tolerances are too fine and the amount of trapping needed depends on the accuracy of the printing press and, in part, on the types of colors and paper used.

Trapping on the desktop does offer advantages: primarily time and money. Whether doing your own trapping will save either depends on how difficult the trapping is, the options you use, and your level of knowledge.

Here are a few pointers:

- Avoid creating situations that require trapping. Some trapping becomes necessary as a result of page design choices, such as abutting or overlapping color areas. If you can avoid these, you won't need to trap them.

- Consider your trapping options: In PageMaker you can trap simple elements. For more complex elements, such as those including multiple lines, you can create the element and add trapping in a drawing program, such as Aldus FreeHand, and then import it as an EPS; ask your prepress service provider to use Aldus TrapWise; or trap traditionally. Sometimes, you'll use more than one of these options. Your prepress service provider can advise you.

- If you're learning about trapping, try trapping simple jobs first, and review your work at each step. Consult with your commercial printer to find out whether your trapping worked. "As a printer, you've got to know the job—before you get to the printing stage—to know if the film looks right," says Zwang.

- Don't assume responsibility for trapping unless you're comfortable with what you're doing, Zwang suggests. It's often less expensive to have a commercial printer do the trapping than to fix incorrect traps late in the production process.

This section explains the choices and printing options that PageMaker offers you when printing spot- and process-color separations of your publications. It also discusses options for proofing your publication, checking your separations, and compressing and handing off files to your prepress service provider.

Print separations one of three ways:

- directly from PageMaker.

- from another desktop post-processing application.

- by using OPI (Open Prepress Interface) to link to a high-end electronic prepress system, such as those manufactured by Linotype-Hell and Scitex. Contact your commercial printer or prepress service provider to learn more about working with these proprietary systems.

Post-processing applications available from Aldus include Aldus PrePrint, an image-enhancement and color-separation tool; Aldus TrapWise, a PostScript-based automatic trapping utility; and Aldus PressWise, an electronic-imposition tool.

Printing separations from PageMaker

Key printing options, and information about selecting screen rulings and angles, choosing the right paper size, and handing off files to a prepress service provider.

Using post-processing applications

Desktop tools available to handle prepress tasks electronically: Aldus TrapWise for trapping, Aldus PressWise for imposition, and Aldus PrePrint for printing separations.

Proofing your publications

Options for previewing and proofing publications, and guidelines for checking your separations.

These pages present key options for printing color separations from PageMaker and general information about setting up PostScript files to work with post-processing applications. To select these options, choose "Print…" from the File menu. See "Working with post-processing applications" on page 58 for more specific information about integrating post-processing applications into your work flow.

Note: PageMaker cannot separate RGB color TIFF images. If your publication contains these types of images, use Aldus PrePrint or another post-processor to create your separations. Reliably creating separations of color PICT files is difficult; for best results, use another graphic format whenever possible.

Print document dialog box

A Select a target printer from the list of installed output devices (Windows only).

B Choose the PPD (PostScript printer description) file for your final printer.

C Select an orientation. The orientation should match that in the "Page setup" dialog box.

D Click to display the "Paper" printing options.

E Click to display the "Options" printing options.

F Click to display the "Color" printing options.

Color printing dialog box

A Click to print spot- and process-color separations.

B A checkmark (Macintosh) or an "X" (Windows) in the "Print" column indicates that the ink will print.

C The "Ink" column lists the names of each spot- and process-color ink needed to print the colors in your publication.

D Select an ink name, and then check this option to print that ink.

E Select the screen ruling and printer resolution recommended by your commercial printer.

F To print right-reading, emulsion-side-down pages, check "Mirror." To print right-reading, emulsion side up, leave "Mirror" unchecked.

G Check to print a negative version of your publication.

H Click to temporarily convert all of the spot colors in your publication (including any spot colors in EPS files) to process colors.

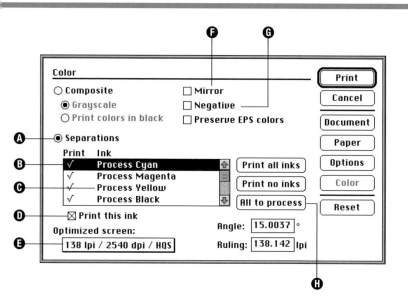

A Print to: Linotronic 530 on FILE:
B Type: Linotronic 530-RIP 30 v52.3

Key Print document options

The most important option you'll select in the "Print document" dialog box is the printer "Type," or PPD file. Included in the PPD file is information about available fonts, predefined paper sizes, and, especially critical for color separations, optimized screens.

Key Color options

The "Color" printing dialog box controls important options for printing color separations from PageMaker. After selecting the "Separations" option, select the inks you want to print and the "Optimized screen" setting recommended by your commercial printer. Don't use "All to process" if you want to print spot-color separations for any spot colors used in your publication.

Options printing dialog box

A

Key Options printing options

Use this dialog box to select marking options for your separations, to control the way TIFF images print, and to print PostScript files to a disk.

A Check "Printer's marks" to print crop marks, registration marks, and density- and color-control bars. Check "Page information" to print separation and filename information, the current date, and the page number on each separation. You need to print on a paper size that's at least .875 inch (23mm) larger than your publication page size to print these marks.

B Always select "Normal" when printing separations directly from PageMaker.

C Select "Omit TIFF files" if you are printing a PostScript file to use with a post-processor with OPI-linking capabilities, such as Aldus PrePrint.

D Check to create a PostScript file of your publication. PageMaker saves the PostScript file in the current folder or directory unless you specify another location by clicking "Save as..." (Macintosh) or "Browse..." (Windows).

E Click to print a standard PostScript file to disk.

F Click to print an EPS file for each page in the selected page range. Aldus TrapWise works with EPS files.

G Click to create an OPI-compatible separation file (SEP), which you can open in Aldus PrePrint or another external post-processor (such as Publisher's Prism from Insight Systems) to print color separations.

Paper printing dialog box

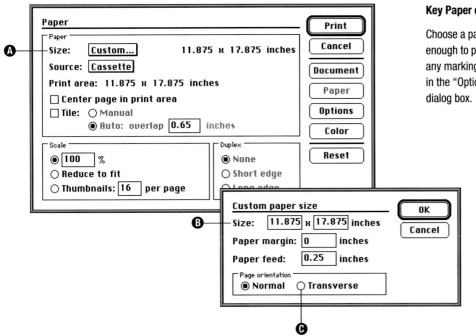

Choose a paper size large enough to print the page and any markings you selected in the "Options" printing dialog box.

A Select the paper (film) size on which you want to print, or select "Custom…" to define a custom paper size. For more information about selecting a paper size, see "Choosing the right paper size" on page 56.

When you select "Custom…" from the "Size" list, the "Custom paper size" dialog box opens. "Custom…" is available only if you select a PPD for an output device that supports the use of custom paper sizes.

B Enter the paper size you wish to use. By default, PageMaker displays the dimensions of your page. If you've selected "Printer's marks" or "Page information," PageMaker automatically increases the paper size to accommodate printer's marks.

C Click to create a transverse page. If the long dimension of the paper is shorter than the width of the media in the output device, you can save paper or film by selecting this option.

Printers simulate a wide range of colors by printing varying-sized dots of the four process-color inks; the pattern of dots for each process-color ink is called a halftone screen. Halftone screens are also used to break continuous-tone art (both black-and-white and color) into a series of dots that re-create the image on the printing press. Two factors—screen ruling and screen angle—determine how these dots of ink print in relation to each other and, as a result, the quality of your final printed piece. The screen ruling specifies how large each dot is, which determines how fine or coarse the image appears; the screen angle is the angle used to print the patterns of dots, which determines the clarity of the resulting color.

PPD files contain optimized screen information for related printers. This information consists of a screen ruling setting and screen angles for each process ink, as well as values used to print spot-color inks. These optimized screens provide the best possible results when printing color separations on PostScript imagesetters.

When you select a PPD file for the "Type" option in the "Print document" dialog box, the optimized screens from that file are listed in the "Optimized screens" option when "Separations" is selected in the "Color" printing dialog box. The overall screen ruling value for an available print resolution appears in the "Optimized screen" listing; the screen angles and rulings for the individual inks appear when you select the individual inks.

Note: If you apply a screen ruling to a TIFF image using the "Image control…" command, that screen ruling takes precedence over the screen ruling you set for your publication.

Guidelines for specifying screen rulings

Screen ruling	Type of paper
65 to 85 lpi	Newsprint and other absorbent, uncoated stock.
90 to 133 lpi	Inexpensive coated stock.
133 to 150 lpi	Medium- and high-quality coated stocks running on fast presses.
Up to 200 lpi	High-quality coated stock running on highly accurate presses.

Since both the printing inks and the press play a role in determining the best screen ruling to use, always consult with your commercial printer before specifying the screen ruling.

When you select an "Optimized screen" in the "Color" printing dialog box you can see the screen "Ruling" and "Angle" values assigned to the selected ink.

Screen ruling

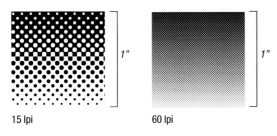

15 lpi

60 lpi

Screen ruling, measured in lines per inch (lpi), is the number of lines (or rows) of halftone dots printed per inch on the page. (Screen ruling is also called linescreen or screen frequency.) A high screen ruling prints the dots close together, creating sharp, distinct colors and images. A low screen ruling prints the dots farther apart, creating a coarser effect.

Because different types of paper absorb inks differently, the characteristics of your paper generally determine the screen ruling you should use.

Screen angle

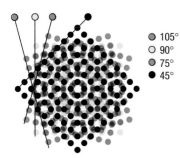

○ 105°
○ 90°
○ 75°
● 45°

Together, the screen angles for the individual inks produce a rosette pattern.

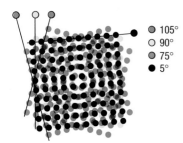

○ 105°
○ 90°
○ 75°
● 5°

When the angle of a process ink is incorrect, an undesirable pattern called a moiré results.

In commercial printing, the lines of dots in the halftone screens for each process-color ink are positioned at a particular angle, ensuring that the halftone dots for each ink print in a rosette pattern that helps create the illusion of multiple colors. Traditionally, the cyan screen is printed at 105°, the magenta screen at 75°, the yellow screen at 90°, and the black screen at 45°. Because imagesetters simulate halftone dots by grouping printer dots together in halftone cells, producing consistent angles at 75° and 105° has been difficult.

Several screening-technology solutions address this problem. Rational Tangent (RT) screening, developed by Linotype-Hell and available on all PostScript imagesetters, uses empirically determined screen ruling and angle combinations that approximate the traditional combinations to print halftone screens. Adobe's Accurate Screens, Agfa's Balanced Screen Technology (BST), and Linotype-Hell's HQS Screening (HQS) are available on imagesetters with specific PostScript RIPs (raster image processors); all are closer to the traditional screen ruling angle combination than RT screens, and therefore offer better results.

In general, you print on a paper size that matches your page size. However, when printing separations, you also want to print the filename, the separation name, crop marks, color- and density-control bars on each page—which means you must use a paper size .875 inch (23mm) larger than your page size.

In the "Paper" printing dialog box, the "Size" list displays paper sizes defined in the selected PPD. If the selected printer type supports custom paper sizes (most imagesetters do, most low-resolution desktop printers don't), "Custom…" is also available. Most imagesetters define regular paper sizes (such as letter and tabloid) and "Transverse" paper sizes (regular paper sizes that are rotated 90° when printed in order to make more efficient use of imagesetter media). You can select a predefined paper size or select "Custom…" in the "Size" list to create a custom paper size for your job. To create a custom paper size that displays in the "Size" list in any PageMaker publication, create a custom printer file as described in "Creating a custom printer file" on page 70.

Note: For many jobs, the paper or film you output is combined, or stripped, into a larger page of film, from which the printing plates are made. Your pre-press service provider may use Aldus PressWise to automate this task. See "Using a post-processor for trapping and imposition" on page 60 for additional information.

▶ **To select the right paper size**

1. **In the "Print document" dialog box select the "Orientation" option that matches your page setup.**

2. **In the "Paper" printing dialog box, select or create a paper size that meets your needs.**

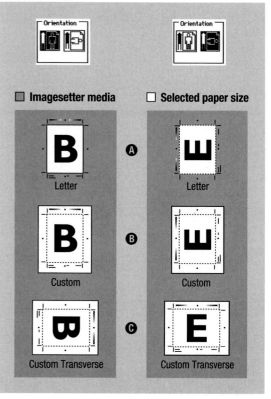

A When your paper size exactly matches your page size, printer's marks and bleeds do not print.

B Create a custom paper size .875 inch (23mm) larger in each dimension than your publication page in order to accommodate printer's marks.

C If the long dimension of your paper size is smaller than the width of the imagesetter media, select "Transverse" in the "Custom paper size" dialog box, or select a "Transverse" paper size from the "Size" list in the "Paper" printing dialog box.

▶ To save your publication for remote printing

1. Choose "Save as…" from the File menu.

Choosing "Save as…" also reduces the file size by deleting mini-save information stored in the file.

2. Specify a new folder or directory, then check "Files required for remote printing" or "All linked files."

Specifying "Files required for remote printing" copies the publication and linked files not stored in the publication to the destination folder or directory. Specifying "All linked files" copies the publication and all internally and externally linked files to the destination folder or directory.

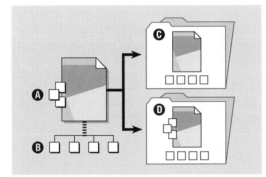

A Linked files can be stored internally (a copy of the file is stored in the publication) or…

B …linked files can be stored externally (PageMaker stores a screen image of the file only, and links to the original graphic file on a disk).

C Select "Files required for remote printing" to copy only externally linked graphic files when you "Save as" or…

D …select "All linked files" to copy all internally and externally linked text and graphics files.

3. Click "Save."

Hand off the folder or directory containing both the publication and the linked files to your prepress service provider.

The diagram on this page illustrates the process of handing off a PageMaker publication with externally linked graphics files to a prepress service provider.

Choosing "Save as…" compresses PageMaker files to their minimum size. You may also want to use a compression utility, such as Stuffit from Aladdin Systems (Macintosh) or PKZip from PKWare (Windows), to further compress large files before you hand them off. Use the file-compression utility recommended by your prepress service provider.

Always discuss handoffs with your prepress service provider; you may be asked to provide a PostScript file containing all linked files, your PageMaker publication and any linked files, or both. If you print your publication to a disk as a PostScript file, internally and externally linked files can be automatically included. For more information, see "Managing links" on page 37.

To save time and money in the prepress process, or for those times when PageMaker's color-separation options do not meet all of your needs, you may want to talk to your prepress service provider about using PostScript-based post-processing applications, such as Aldus PrePrint, Aldus PressWise, and Aldus TrapWise. Having a prepress service provider handle prepress tasks using post-processing applications adds the benefit of their professional expertise to the prepress process, and makes it easier for design professionals to work in their areas of expertise.

For example, your prepress service provider might incorporate these tools into the prepress workflow:

- when your publication contains certain types of imported graphics, such as RGB TIFFs, that PageMaker cannot separate.

- to automatically create traps for your PageMaker pages or to trap illustrations created with Post-Script-based illustration tools, such as Aldus FreeHand.

- to handle complex stripping and imposition tasks (to save the cost of manually assembling multiple pages on one sheet of film prior to creating the plates used in commercial printing).

After discussing your project with your commercial printer and prepress service provider, determine which prepress tasks can be done electronically, which are most cost-effective to do manually, who will be responsible for each task, and which desktop post-processing applications will be used. If necessary, talk with a color prepress house to determine whether to do your separations on the desktop or using a high-end color system.

Post-processors and the prepress workflow

This diagram provides an overview of the four phases of the prepress process, and outlines both the tools available to complete each task and the respective roles of both designers and prepress service providers.

Depending on your schedule, budget, and the requirements for each publication you design, prepress tasks (trapping, creating impositions, and printing separations) can be accomplished either within PageMaker or by using post-processing applications.

Having the tools to do prepress tasks doesn't mean you should necessarily assume the responsibility. Desktop tools have expanded the role of designers; if you're new to the prepress process, consider hiring a prepress service provider to handle these tasks.

You'll find more information about desktop-based post-processing tools available for trapping, creating impositions, and printing separations on the following pages.

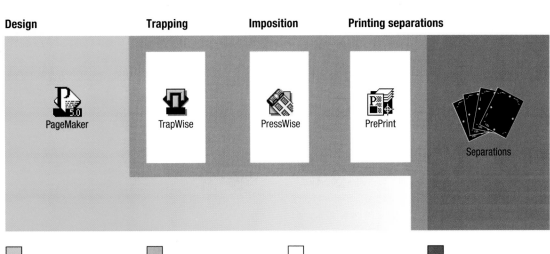

Design **Trapping** **Imposition** **Printing separations**

PageMaker   TrapWise   PressWise   PrePrint   Separations

The yellow area illustrates the expanding role of designers in the prepress workflow.

The light blue area represents the tasks that are traditionally performed by prepress professionals.

Electronic tools used by prepress service providers are located in the white areas.

Both the prepress workflow and the tools used to handle prepress tasks are evolving rapidly; the end result of the prepress process is a set of separations used to produce the plates needed to print on a commercial printing press.

Trapping your publications

Aldus TrapWise traps objects on your PageMaker pages accurately and quickly. Because TrapWise can trap selected portions of an object, it is preferable to the object-based trapping found in most other PostScript-based page-layout and illustration programs (pages 44-45 explain how to create simple, object-based traps in PageMaker). And because TrapWise traps an EPS file automatically, it eliminates both the possibility of trapping errors and the time-consuming labor needed to manually create object-based traps.

Use TrapWise when your publication requires professional-quality trapping. To prepare a PageMaker publication for trapping in Aldus TrapWise, print the pages you wish to trap to disk as EPS files.

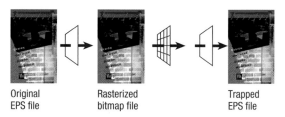

Original   Rasterized   Trapped
EPS file   bitmap file   EPS file

TrapWise works by turning EPS images into high-resolution rasterized bitmaps, calculating the necessary traps, and then amending a copy of the EPS file with PostScript describing the traps. Once your files have been trapped, use PageMaker or Aldus PrePrint to separate them (use PrePrint if the EPS file contains externally linked images).

Creating imposition layouts

Stripping pages together to create imposition layouts, another prepress task, is easily accomplished by Aldus PressWise. Traditionally, film separations are manually fastened together in the position in which they will print. The resulting flat is used to make plates for the printing press.

The "Build booklet…" Addition included with PageMaker can create simple four-up impositions. If you're unfamiliar with traditional imposition practices or if your jobs require more complex imposition layouts ask your prepress service provider to use Aldus PressWise. To create a layout imposition of your PageMaker publication, your prepress service provider will print your file to a disk as a PostScript file for separations (SEP), open it in PressWise, and create the imposition layout.

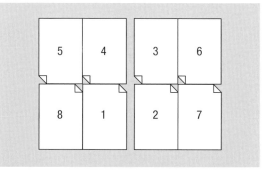

This is a work-and-turn imposition layout for an eight-page signature. Once assembled in this layout, the pages for a single color job are printed at high resolution to a single sheet of film. For color work, the imposition layout is printed to disk as a PostScript (SEP) file and Aldus PrePrint is used to print separations of the imposition.

Downloading fonts from PrePrint

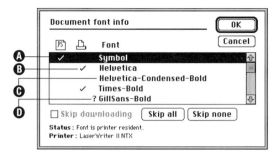

Aldus PrePrint's "Document font info" dialog box lets you verify that your fonts print correctly by listing all fonts in your SEP file and indicating whether the fonts: (A) are included in the SEP file, (B) are resident in the printer (based on the font information in the PPD file selected in PrePrint), (C) are available for downloading, or (D) are missing, and therefore need to be located before the separations will print correctly.

Printing linked graphics from PrePrint

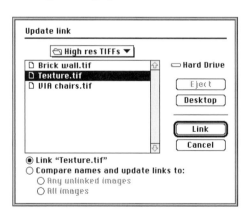

Aldus PrePrint reads the OPI comments in a SEP file to identify images and their positions within your publication. As long as the image files will be available when you print from PrePrint, there's no need to increase the size of your SEP file by including images when printing to a disk from PageMaker. Refer to the *PrePrint 1.5 User Manual* for more information.

Use Aldus PrePrint to create separations of your PageMaker publications when:

- you want to use PrePrint's tools to enhance continuous-tone art included in your publication.

- you want to use PrePrint's press controls—including dot gain and gray component replacement (GCR)—to adjust your separations.

- you've used Aldus PressWise to create layout impositions of a color publication.

- your publication contains RGB TIFF images. PageMaker can separate CMYK TIFF and DCS images, but not RGB TIFF images.

Before you can use Aldus PrePrint to create separations, you need to create a PostScript (SEP) file in PageMaker for separations. Select your PageMaker printing options carefully, making sure that:

- linked files, especially externally linked scanned graphics, are available.

- the right PPD file is selected for "Type" in the "Print document" dialog box.

- fonts needed to print text within EPS graphics are available (Windows only). PrePrint's "Document font info" dialog box does not list fonts in nested PostScript files.

Aldus PrePrint is available on the Macintosh. If you're working with PageMaker for Windows, use a file transfer utility to transfer the SEP file you create in Windows to the Macintosh.

Note: Use a desktop link to a high-end color electronic publishing system, such as Linotype-Hell's ScriptMaster, when you want to take advantage of the drum scanners and image-manipulation software available on those proprietary systems.

As a matter of course, you should review your publication throughout its development to:

- check the layout.

- anticipate and solve costly and time-consuming prepress and production problems, such as moiré patterns and trapping problems.

- verify the accuracy of printed colors.

These pages present the options for reviewing and proofing your PageMaker publications from least (left) to most reliable (right). In general, the more closely the proofing method mimics the conditions of the actual printing press, the more reliably it will indicate the final product's quality. More reliable proofs are also more expensive.

You can correct problems identified in an early review easily; the same problem identified on separations will be time-consuming and expensive to fix. Correction costs continue to increase from this point—errors discovered during a press check are the most expensive to fix. Intersperse review and proofing cycles into your development cycle, and, for color work, plan to create separation-based proofs.

The proofing process

On-screen previews

Black-and-white comps

Evaluate your publication on-screen throughout the design process to check the overall layout and to refine the appearance of text.

Don't rely on the on-screen appearance of colors to proof your colors: colors on the screen rarely match exactly their final printed appearance. Calibrated monitors offer improved color display but are still no substitute for a more reliable color proofing method.

Black-and-white composites let you review your layout and text, and low-resolution separations let you verify that objects and inks are printing on the correct separations. PostScript printers can also alert you to problems you may encounter on an imagesetter—files that generate PostScript errors on a desktop printer usually cause problems on an imagesetter as well.

Tip

To proof only the text in your publication, or to troubleshoot printing problems with imported graphics by isolating the problem graphics, select "Proof print" in the "Print" dialog box. When this option is selected, PageMaker substitutes a box with an "X" in it for all imported graphics.

Color comps

Separation-based proofs

Overlay proof   Laminated proof

Press check

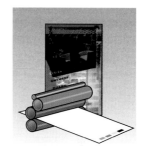

Color composites, especially useful for previewing overall page design and for basic color forecasting, range in quality from low-resolution color halftones to continuous-tone dye sublimation prints.

Because the actual separations from which the plates are created are not used, these composites have two critical limitations as a proofing method: color accuracy (even on high-resolution output) is limited and common press problems, such as moirés and trapping, cannot be detected.

Next to a press check, separation-based color proofs are the most accurate proofs available, and are considered the industry standard. Because these composite proofs are created from the separations used to create plates, they provide a reliable method for color forecasting and for identifying areas in your design that may cause problems on the press.

Overlay proofs, such as DuPont Cromacheck and 3M Color Key, are created by printing the separations on acetate sheets colored to match the four process inks; the sheets are then layered on top of each other. Overlay proofs are an economical way to check the placement of objects, verify that objects overprint and knock out as specified, and confirm that traps print correctly; they are less reliable than laminated proofs for proofing final colors.

Laminated (or integral) proofs, such as Fuji ColorArt, DuPont Cromalin, and 3M Matchprint, are created by representing each separation on a layer of pigmented material, and then binding the pigmented layers together (keep in mind that unless the base material for the proof is your paper, the printed colors may look slightly different). Laminated proofs are a reliable method for color forecasting and for identifying moiré problems.

A press check is the only way to see the true effects of color on the paper you've selected. For a press check, the printer sets up the press for the actual print run using plates made from your approved separations.

Once the press is adjusted and you approve a press sample, the printer begins the final press run. The printer then compares the approved press sample with the final printed pages throughout the press run to ensure consistent quality.

Checking separation accuracy

The success of your print job depends in large part on the quality of your film separations. When you select a commercial printer, discuss who's responsible for checking the separations. Either you or your prepress service provider must check that:

• the dimensions of the publication are correct.

• all objects printed on the correct separations.

• objects overprinted and knocked out correctly.

• all fonts printed correctly.

• bleed objects extend beyond the boundary indicated by the crop marks.

• areas you expected to trap actually do trap.

• all the separations printed as specified and with the necessary printer's marks aligned correctly.

• overlapping process-color separations create a rosette pattern and do not show unacceptable moiré patterns (yellow always creates a moiré pattern).

• tints and halftones (including scanned images) look consistent and smooth.

Checking film quality

Certain tasks necessary for checking separations require specific equipment, such as a densitometer and a tool for measuring screen angle and ruling. You may want to rely on your service bureau or commercial printer to check:

• the overall quality of the film separations. Look for streaking, scratches, or other damage to the film, and make sure that areas that should be clear aren't foggy.

• the maximum density (Dmax) of the black areas on your film separations.

• that the dot value of your tints and halftones is correct.

• that the screen angle and ruling for each separation printed as specified.

Tip

When proofing separations on a light table, tape the magenta separation down first and then place the black, cyan, and yellow separations on top in ascending order. Any moiré that appears in your film separations will look worse than the moiré in your final printed piece because the black in the color separations is darker than the individual inks.

With more prepress work being performed on the desktop, printing professionals often have less control over how print jobs are constructed. Traditional strippers typically have years of training, union proficiency requirements, or on-the-job experience, but anyone can do color separation, trapping, or imposition on the desktop, consultant Chuck Weger says. "It's empowering, but it also makes it harder to prevent mistakes."

As the former manager of advanced technologies at a large Washington, D.C., printing firm, and now based in Alexandria, Virginia, Weger guided his company's transition from exclusively traditional stripping to a mix of electronic and traditional prepress. Communication with your commercial printer at all production stages is important, and communication at the handoff stage is absolutely essential, he says.

At the handoff stage, Weger suggests watching for several trouble spots:

- Pretest new techniques. "About 25% of all desktop jobs involve some new process or software," Weger estimates. "The handoff is not the place to be trying something you haven't done before."

- Determine who is responsible for checking the settings in printing dialog boxes. This is where problems with incorrect screen settings, scaling (typically because you scaled the publication to print proofs on a laser printer), incorrect target printers (your laser printer again), and crop marks occur.

- Similarly, decide who is responsible for quality control before outputting the publication. For example, talk with your printer early in the design stage to determine if your file will need trapping. If it does, decide who will do the trapping and who will verify that the traps work properly. "Trapping is where a lot of finger-pointing happens," Weger says. "Rather than taking a file apart to determine and correct potential trapping problems, we prefer to do the detective work up-front." You may decide to have the prepress service provider do the trapping, either electronically or traditionally, but in any case you need to plan accordingly.

- Discuss your color choices before you begin serious work. If you use spot colors, make sure you and your commercial printer know how you expect them to be printed—as true spot colors (requiring a separation page and ink for each color), or approximated, using process colors.

In general, a smooth handoff to a commercial printer depends on the communication and planning that comes before the handoff. "The earlier you catch an error, the cheaper it is to correct," Weger says. "Invest time and money in early quality control. If it means inventing imaginary schedules for other people in the organization to get their work in on time, then do that. It's like setting your watch ahead five minutes."

This section discusses how to create two types of files in order to customize PageMaker's working environment: custom printer files and color library files.

You can create custom printer files to supplement the font and paper size information in PostScript printer description (PPD) files. PPD files provide key information about your printer used by PageMaker when printing.

You can also create your own custom color library files to use in addition to the color-matching system libraries included with PageMaker.

Working with PostScript printer description files

A tour of a PPD (PostScript printer description) file and instructions for creating a custom printer file for your printer.

Creating custom color libraries

How to create custom color libraries and an overview of the Aldus color file (ACF) file format.

PageMaker uses PostScript printer description (PPD) files when you print on a PostScript printer. PostScript printer description files describe the standard features available on a printer, including:

- the amount of memory available.

- predefined paper sizes.

- resident fonts.

- optimized screens, used to print color separations.

PageMaker uses the information in the PPD file to determine what PostScript information to send to the printer when you print a publication. For example, PageMaker assumes that the fonts listed in your PPD file reside in the printer, so they are not downloaded when you print.

If you install additional fonts or memory, you must create a custom printer file that supplements your printer's PPD file. The following pages explain how to create a custom printer file.

Macintosh note: Custom printer files have the same function as and take the place of the PDX files included with PageMaker 4.2.

Understanding printer files

Although you shouldn't modify PPD files, it's helpful to know a little bit about their structure. The callouts to the sample PPD on the facing page highlight key features.

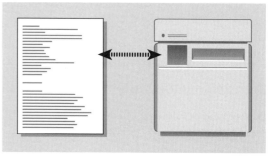

PPD (PostScript printer description) files describe the fonts, paper sizes, and resolution capabilities that are standard for your printer.

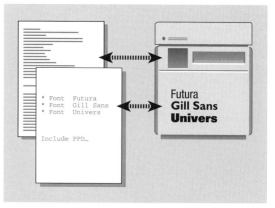

If you add printer-resident fonts, or want to define custom paper sizes, you can create a custom printer file to supplement your printer's PPD file.

For more information…

PageMaker 5.0 User Manual

"Understanding PPD files" 209

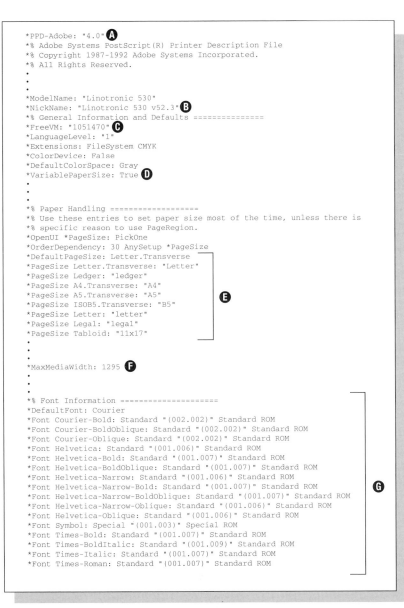

```
*PPD-Adobe: "4.0" Ⓐ
*% Adobe Systems PostScript(R) Printer Description File
*% Copyright 1987-1992 Adobe Systems Incorporated.
*% All Rights Reserved.
•
•
*ModelName: "Linotronic 530"
*NickName: "Linotronic 530 v52.3" Ⓑ
*% General Information and Defaults ===============
*FreeVM: "1051470" Ⓒ
*LanguageLevel: "1"
*Extensions: FileSystem CMYK
*ColorDevice: False
*DefaultColorSpace: Gray
*VariablePaperSize: True Ⓓ
•
•
•
*% Paper Handling ====================
*% Use these entries to set paper size most of the time, unless there is
*% specific reason to use PageRegion.
*OpenUI *PageSize: PickOne
*OrderDependency: 30 AnySetup *PageSize
*DefaultPageSize: Letter.Transverse
*PageSize Letter.Transverse: "Letter"
*PageSize Ledger: "ledger"
*PageSize A4.Transverse: "A4"
*PageSize A5.Transverse: "A5"
*PageSize ISOB5.Transverse: "B5"
*PageSize Letter: "letter"
*PageSize Legal: "legal"
*PageSize Tabloid: "11x17"
•
•
•
*MaxMediaWidth: 1295 Ⓕ
•
•
•
*% Font Information =====================
*DefaultFont: Courier
*Font Courier-Bold: Standard "(002.002)" Standard ROM
*Font Courier-BoldOblique: Standard "(002.002)" Standard ROM
*Font Courier-Oblique: Standard "(002.002)" Standard ROM
*Font Helvetica: Standard "(001.006)" Standard ROM
*Font Helvetica-Bold: Standard "(001.007)" Standard ROM
*Font Helvetica-BoldOblique: Standard "(001.007)" Standard ROM
*Font Helvetica-Narrow: Standard "(001.006)" Standard ROM
*Font Helvetica-Narrow-Bold: Standard "(001.007)" Standard ROM
*Font Helvetica-Narrow-BoldOblique: Standard "(001.007)" Standard ROM
*Font Helvetica-Narrow-Oblique: Standard "(001.006)" Standard ROM
*Font Helvetica-Oblique: Standard "(001.006)" Standard ROM
*Font Symbol: Special "(001.003)" Special ROM
*Font Times-Bold: Standard "(001.007)" Standard ROM
*Font Times-BoldItalic: Standard "(001.009)" Standard ROM
*Font Times-Italic: Standard "(001.007)" Standard ROM
*Font Times-Roman: Standard "(001.007)" Standard ROM
```

A Indicates the version number of the PPD file. PageMaker 5.0 uses PPD version 4.0 files.

B By default, PageMaker for Windows displays the PPD nickname in the "Type" list in the "Print document" dialog box.

C "FreeVM" states in bytes the amount of memory available in the standard version of your printer.

D "VariablePaperSize: True" or "CustomPaper: True" indicate that your printer supports custom paper sizes.

E The PPD file lists the standard paper sizes available for your printer.

F "MaxMediaWidth" states the maximum paper or film width that your imagesetter can use.

G The PPD file lists the standard, built-in fonts for your printer.

The easiest way to create a custom printer file is to use the "Update PPD…" Addition (included with PageMaker 5.0 for the Macintosh). The "Update PPD…" Addition determines which printer you have chosen in PageMaker's "Print" dialog box and uses the information provided by this printer—a list of printer-resident fonts, the amount of available printer memory, and a standard list of extra paper sizes—to create a custom printer file on your hard drive. For more information on using this Addition, refer to *Aldus PageMaker 5.0 Online Help.*

If you are using PageMaker for Windows or have not installed the "Update PPD…" Addition, you can use the PPDSHELL.PS file and the procedure outlined on the following page to create a custom printer file. The custom printer file created using this procedure contains the same information as the one created using the "Update PPD…" Addition.

Using the PPDSHELL.PS file is a two-step process. You first download the PPDSHELL.PS file to your PostScript printer to create a custom printer file. Then you link the custom printer to your printer's PPD file by opening the custom printer file in a text-editing program and entering the PPD filename for your printer. When you select the custom printer file in PageMaker, both the custom printer file and the PPD file are read.

Windows note: Because the Windows printer driver does not support two-way communication between your printer and computer, you will need to copy the PPDSHELL.PS file to a Macintosh computer and download it from there. Then, copy the custom printer file to the PPD4 directory on your Windows-compatible computer. You can select the custom printer file from PageMaker for Windows the next time you print.

Specifying custom paper sizes

Your custom printer file includes a list of standard extra paper sizes. There are two ways to create your own custom paper sizes in PageMaker:

• Define a custom paper size in the new "Custom paper size" dialog box in PageMaker. (Choose "Custom…" for "Size" in the "Paper" print dialog box.) The paper size you create is saved with the publication, so you can use that size any time you print the publication.

• Create a custom paper size and save it as a printer style using the "Printer styles…" Addition. You can use the style you create with any publication. Simply print using the "Printer styles…" Addition and apply the style with the custom paper size to publications in the print queue. For more information, see "Printer styles…" in *Aldus Additions for PageMaker 5.0.*

▶ To create a custom printer file manually

Windows note: Copy the PPDSHELL.PS file to a Macintosh and follow the instructions below. The PPDSHELL.PS file is located in the UTILITY\PS_TOOLS directory in the language subdirectory (USENGLSH, for example) of the Aldus directory.

1. **Set up your printer.**

   Open the Chooser, and select the LaserWriter icon. Select your printer, and then close the Chooser to save your changes.

2. **Doubie-click to open the LaserWriter Font Utility.**

   If you're using the LaserWriter 7.X (or earlier) printer driver, use any version of the LaserWriter Font Utility. When using the LaserWriter 8.0 (or later) printer driver, you must use the LaserWriter Font Utility 7.4 (or later). The LaserWriter Font Utility is located on the System 7 "Tidbits" disk.

3. **Choose "Download PostScript File" from the Utilities menu.**

4. **Locate and select the PPDSHELL.PS file, and then click "OK" to download it.**

5. **Specify a filename and location for the custom printer file created by PPDSHELL.PS, and click "OK."**

   The PPDSHELL.PS file downloads to your printer and creates a custom printer file as the output log file. The filename identifies the custom printer file in Macintosh PageMaker. PageMaker for Windows uses the custom printer filename when "Display PPD name" is checked in the "Preferences" dialog box.

6. **Quit the LaserWriter Font Utility.**

▶ To link the custom printer file and PPD file

1. **Open the custom printer file in a text-editing program, such as TeachText.**

2. **Type the name of your printer's PPD file at the "*Include:" line.**

   The "*Include:" line links your custom printer file to a standard PPD file. Replace the placeholder PPD name with the name of your printer's PPD file using straight (not typographer's) quotation marks around the filename. *Windows note:* Filenames of the PPD files are listed in the PPDLIST.WRI file located in the UTILITY directory.

   ```
   *% Include Statement
   *% ==============================
   *Include: "Printer.PPD"
   *% End of Aldus PostScript(R) Printer
   Description Including File.
   ```

3. **Save the custom printer file.**

   Save the custom printer file as a text-only file in the same folder as your PPD files. To use the custom printer file with PageMaker for Windows, copy it to a Windows-compatible computer, place it in the PPD4 directory in the language subdirectory (USENGLSH, for example) of the Aldus directory, and select the custom printer file as you would a PPD file.

Macintosh note: If you have used the LaserWriter 7.X (or earlier) printer driver, be sure to select the LaserWriter 8.0 icon (or the Adobe PSWriter icon) in the Chooser to set up your printer for PageMaker 5.0. For details, see "Setting up a PostScript printer on the Macintosh" on page 205 of *PageMaker 5.0 User Manual.*

▶ To create a custom color library

To make specifying the same colors in different publications easier, you can create a custom color library from a publication's "Colors" palette using the "Create color library..." Addition (refer to *Aldus Additions for PageMaker 5.0* for more information). You can also create color libraries from scratch using the standard Aldus color file (ACF) format described on these two pages.

1. Open the sample CRAYON.ACF file in a text-editing program.

The CRAYON.ACF file is installed in the Color folder or directory in the Aldus folder or directory.

2. Add values to the key words in the file.

All of the key words must appear in the file in the order shown in the sample file to the right, even if you do not include values for them. Callouts on the facing page provide more information about each key word.

3. Save the file as a text file.

Make sure that the file is in the Color folder or directory in the Aldus folder or directory and that ACF is specified as the filename extension.

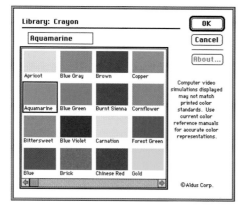

```
ACF 1.0  Ⓐ
Crayon  Ⓑ
LibraryVersion: 1.0  Ⓒ
Copyright: ©Aldus Corp.  Ⓓ
AboutMessage:  Ⓔ
Names: Partial  Ⓕ
Rows: 4  Ⓖ
Columns: 4  Ⓗ
Entries: 62  Ⓘ
Prefix:  Ⓙ
Suffix:
Type: Spot  Ⓚ
Models: CMYK RGB  Ⓛ
PreferredModel: RGB  Ⓜ
Data:  Ⓝ
0 0.15 0.3 0
65535 55705 45875
Apricot

1.0 0.1 0.1 0
0 58982 58982
Aquamarine

0.15 0.7 1.0 0
55705 19661 0
Bittersweet
```

A ACF 1.0 Identifies the library to PageMaker.

B Type a name for your library (up to 31 characters). The name you specify appears in the "Library" menu in the "Define colors" dialog box.

C LibraryVersion: Type a version number for your library (value optional).

D Copyright: Type any necessary copyright information (value optional).

E AboutMessage: Type text to appear when you click "About" in the "Library" window (value optional).

F Names: Type *Full* to display color names with their prefixes and suffixes. Type *Partial* to display color names only. Type *None* to hide color names.

G Rows: Enter a value between 1 and 10 to specify the number of rows that appear in the "Library" window.

H Columns: Enter a value between 1 and 10 to specify the number of columns that appear in the "Library" window.

I Entries: Type a value indicating the total number of colors in your library.

J Prefix: and/or **Suffix:** Type a prefix (up to 11 characters) and/or a suffix to be included with each color name when the value for "Names" is "Full" (values optional).

K Type: Enter *Spot* to define a library of spot colors, or *Process* for a process color library.

L Models: Enter *CMYK* if you want to define colors by their CMYK (printed) components, and/or *RGB* if you want to define colors for accurate display on-screen. The order in which you list the models is the order in which you'll need to specify the values for each color.

M PreferredModel: Enter *CMYK* or *RGB* to determine which color model is shown by default in the "Edit color" dialog box.

N Data: Define and name colors for your library. If you are using the CMYK model, specify the values for cyan, magenta, yellow, and black from 0-1, where 0 = 0% of the ink and 1 = 100% of the ink. For RGB, specify the values for red, green, and blue as 0-65535 where 0 = 0% and 65535 = 100%. Type the color name (up to 17 characters) below the CMYK and/or RGB values.

Writers: Whitney McCleary and Ellen Wixted, with Kathleen King; interviews by James Larkin

Technical Editor: Barbara Roll

Copy Editor: Margy Kotick

Proofreader: Janice Bultmann

Indexer: Kristen Laine

Designer: Susan Bari Price

Illustrator and Production Lead: Julie Brockmeyer

Production Artist: Laurie Becharas

Production Coordinator: Pamela Hidaka

Prepress Production: Paul Carew

VIA Poster Design: Paul Piacitelli

Special thanks to Rick Fickel and Ray Johnson of Impression Northwest

This book was produced on Apple Macintosh computers using Aldus PageMaker, Aldus FreeHand, Aldus TrapWise, Aldus PressWise, Aldus PrePrint, Adobe Photoshop, Exposure Pro, and Tiffany.

Planning: Our main goal was to present information visually. In addition, we designed the book so that any text to be translated is on the black separation, thus making it possible for Aldus Europe to print the color pages for 17 languages simultaneously. By following the processes described in this book, we were able to manage our costs, the schedule, and the quality.

Communication with our printer: Many design decisions were influenced by our printer's input early in the process. The initial design reviewed by our printer included color bars that crossed the gutter in a spread. This design element was problematic for two reasons: First, holding a consistent color across a spread is difficult, and holding the screened-back color across the gutter might have sacrificed other colors in the illustrations. Second, the color bars on facing pages would be difficult to align exactly when the book was assembled. To minimize these problems, we changed the page design, making the color bars vertical and moving them to the edge of the pages. On the contents pages, where colored lines cross from one page to another, we sidestepped the problem by positioning another element behind the lines in order to camouflage imperfect alignment.

Colors used: In addition to the four process inks, we used PANTONE 5135 as a spot ink. The color bars on each page were defined using cyan, magenta, and yellow, which minimized the need for trapping and reduced total ink coverage. The images on the contents pages were created in Photoshop; three-color grays were used to add color depth and eliminate the need to trap the colored lines.

Graphics: The full-color images were scanned on a Crosfield scanner and saved as CMYK TIFF files. To create the sample poster, these images were combined with several monochrome bitmap images with colors applied in PageMaker. The VIA logo and the patterned background, along with most of the other illustrations, were created and trapped in Aldus FreeHand and exported as EPS files. Exposure Pro (Macintosh) and Tiffany (Windows) were used for screen shots.

To minimize the size of the sample publication file, the color TIFF images were stored externally. EPS images and smaller bitmaps were stored internally.

Trapping: Traps for many of the EPS files (such as those on pages 6 and 15) were created in Aldus FreeHand. Aldus TrapWise was used to trap the illustrations on pages 10, 11, 16-17, 43, and 59.

Proofing: Apple LaserWriter II NTX PostScript printers were used for daily proofs and test separations. The QMS ColorScript Model 30 and the Canon CLC 500 with EFI's Fiery RIP v125i were used for low-resolution color checks. Prior to handing off the publication files, all grayscale art was proofed at 2400 dpi. Fuji's ColorArt system was used to create color proofs; complex spreads (pages 16-17 and 30-31) were proofed twice to verify corrections.

Printing separations: Separations were printed from Aldus PrePrint to an Agfa Proset 9800 at 2400 dpi.

T

"Target printer..." command 28
Target printer, printing problems 39
Terminology, color printing 12–15
TIFF image. *See also* Bitmap image
   applying screen rulings to 36, 54
   RGB TIFF image 50
   scanning 34–37
Tint
   defined 12
   and imagesetter calibration 24
   reason for using 12, 42
Trapping
   bitmap image to colored back-
     ground 45
   chokes 41
   colors, troubleshooting 43–45
   defined 15
   misregistration, compensating
     for 18, 40
   objects 40–46
   in PageMaker 43–45
   process colors 43
   using TrapWise 60
   specifying traps 40
   spreads 41
   trap size guidelines 41
Troubleshooting
   Courier font substituted 39
   file size
     publication file size 57
     scanned image files too large 34
   font problems 38–39
   gaps between overlapping colors 18
   linked graphics 37
   misregistration 14–15
   overscanning image files 34–35
   preventing moiré patterns 18
   printing
     colors do not print well 43–46
     fonts don't print 38–39, 39
   separations
     misregistration 18
     moiré patterns, prevent-
       ing 18, 31
TrueType fonts 38
Trumatch color library 22, 32

U

UCR (under-color removal) 13

W

Web-fed press 17, 23
Wide page orientation 28, 56
WIN.INI file, fonts in 38
"Write PostScript to file" option 52